# JOHN
# WORSLEY'S WAR

# JOHN WORSLEY'S WAR

John Worsley and Kenneth Giggal

**Airlife**
England

**ERRATUM**

The captions on pages 40, 41, 42 have been transposed. They should read as follows:

P.40  AFTER MAST, HMS *DEVONSHIRE*.
P.41  *DEVONSHIRE*'S WALRUS SEAPLANE MOUNTED ON ITS CATAPULT.
P.42  AFTER A FLIGHT THE WALRUS HAD TO BE HOISTED BACK ON BOARD.

Copyright © 1993 by John Worsley and Kenneth Giggal

First published in the UK in 1993
by Airlife Publishing Ltd.

**British Library Cataloguing in Publication Data**
  A catalogue record for this book
  is available from the British Library

ISBN 1 85310 257 1

Printed by Livesey Ltd., Shrewsbury.

# Airlife Publishing Ltd

101 Longden Road, Shrewsbury SY3 9EB.

# Contents

# Photo Credits

The bulk of the illustrations used in this book come from John Worsley's collection, others are by permission of the following:

Peter Chasseaud page 77; Imperial War Museum pages 11, 13, 14, 16 (top), 28, 31, 32, 35, 36, 37, 38, 55, 57, 62, 78, 80, 89, 90, 92, 93, 95, 104, 105, 107, 108; National Maritime Museum pages 83, 84, 87.

The jacket painting is entitled 'St Nazaire Raid March 28 1942'. It shows HMS *Campbeltown* ramming the Normandie Dock Gate. It was commissioned by Lord Newborough (who, at the time of the raid, was Sub Lieut 'Micky' Wynn RNVR in command of MTB74 to the left of the picture) and presented to HM The Queen. It now hangs in HMY *Britannia*.

# CHAPTER 1
# ORIGINS

John Worsley was born in Liverpool on 16 February 1919, the son of an officer in the Royal Navy serving at that time in the shore establishment of that port. When Worsley senior was demobilised six months later he took his new family back to Kabuku, his coffee farm in Kenya some forty miles north of Nairobi.

Worsley remembers his childhood with great affection. Located at an altitude of 6,000 ft amidst beautiful mountain scenery, Kabuku enjoyed a perfect climate and the boy was in his element. At six years old he had his own .22 rifle and hunting around the farm — Kabuku is a Kikuyu word for baby rabbit — was good. He was also allowed to drive the family cars, one of the very first Model T Fords and, later an American Rugby Durant, and trips to Nairobi were guaranteed to provide excitements. There was no paved road between farm and city and so, with the Rugby Durant often stuck in deep mud until hauled clear by the nearest available team of oxen, each trip took one full day.

Great fun for a boy, but in 1928 the bottom dropped out of the coffee market. The Great Recession loomed, and Worsley senior, like so many others, found himself in dire straits. He sent his son home to England, to be lodged at St Wilfrid's school where the fees were subsidised by grants from a Royal Navy Trust. From there, young Worsley won a scholarship to Brighton College, and moved on afterwards to complete his studies at Goldsmith's School of Art. A small legacy of just over £300 gave him £2 per week during his three years at Goldsmith's, and he managed not only to live on this small sum but also to run a car. He invested £4 on an ancient bull-nosed Fiat, and used the old banger to make painting forays along the south coast.

After leaving Goldsmith's he was able to earn a modest living by selling his paintings and sketches to various magazines, neither asking nor expecting any help from his parents. Having salvaged what little they could from Kabuku, they had returned home in 1931 to a life of relative penury. Those good years out in Kenya belonged firmly in the past.

In 1939, the family's lifestyle changed yet again. Worsley senior was recalled to the Navy and assigned to the duty of Passive Defence Officer in Plymouth dockyard. The job-designation was somewhat misleading: he was responsible for all fighting of fires, and the disposal of unexploded bombs.

John Worsley was twenty years old, and eager to get to sea. His father introduced him to an old friend, Captain P. Vivian, R.N.

'ATLANTIC CONVO

# CHAPTER 2
# NORTHERN PATROLS

When Britain and France declared war on Germany on 3 September 1939, Britain was virtually unprepared and Parliament resorted to desperate measures. One of these, an edict known as Article T124, empowered the government to appropriate merchant ships and equip them as AMCs (Armed Merchant Cruisers) under the command of a Royal Navy captain. It was an exercise hastily contrived, and one which resulted in some curious anomalies. Generally, most of the officers and also the guns' crews were regular R.N. or R.N.R. personnel, but once appointed to such a command the captain was responsible for the signing-on of his civilian crew and the recruitment, straight from 'Civvy Street', of several would-be midshipmen. Another odd and even sinister provision of Article T124 was that the merchant seamen *and also the middies* signed on for that ship alone, so that should she be sunk, or survive to be decommissioned, the men would be free to pursue their separate ways. They could stay on the beach, join one or another of the fighting forces, or sign on with a different AMC.

Captain P. Vivian had been given command of the ex-Royal Mail Steamer *Laurentic*, an ageing Cunard White Star liner of 19,000 tons, and was busily converting her into a 'warship' with the emplacement of seven old six-inch guns left over from the 1914–18 war. Four were mounted on the forecastle, three down aft on the poop. Most of his merchant seamen were members of the ship's original complement, which included some 35 Newfoundland fishermen. This left Captain Vivian to find four midshipmen, and John Worsley became one of them.

At that time of frantic preparation, his formal training for service in the Navy occupied just three weeks during which he attended crash-courses on seamanship, gunnery, and the basics of navigation. It was obvious that with such meagre groundings, he must learn as he went along. He joined the now-HMS *Laurentic* at the beginning of October, and was experiencing before the end of that month his first taste of life at sea.

Captain Vivian's orders were to patrol the freezing waters between

Iceland and Greenland to spot, and if possible to sink, any German raider passing through the Denmark Strait *en route* to attack our Atlantic convoys. It was a very tall order for such a vessel. With a top speed of 22 knots, she resembled a block of flats moving slowly across the ocean, and was enormously vulnerable. Her obsolete armament was woefully inadequate against the enemy's modern might. The clumsy six-inchers, with their limited range, were her only defence. She carried no anti-aircraft weapons, no anti-submarine gear, and of course no ASDIC or radar.

Although her first patrol was uneventful, *Laurentic* had a narrow escape. Each patrol around Iceland and Greenland lasted about four weeks, after which it was necessary to return to her base at Liverpool in order to take on coal. *Laurentic* was due to be relieved by HMS *Rawalpindi* an ex-P&O liner of 16,000 tons armed with six six-inch guns, on 23 November. For reasons now obscure, *Rawalpindi* arrived on station three days early, and it was on the 23rd that she came into contact with two new German battlecruisers, the *Scharnhorst* and the *Gneisenau*.

The old P&O liner was commanded by Captain Kennedy (father of the broadcaster Ludovic) who, knowing that his ship stood no chance against the *Scharnhorst's* huge main battery of nine eleven-inch guns, attempted to save the lives of his crew by sheering off to port. That was when he sighted *Gneisenau*, the *Scharnhorst's* twin sister ship, and realising he was trapped between the two, he immediately opened fire. The ensuing battle was ridiculously one-sided. Within a matter of minutes, HMS *Rawalpindi* was ablaze, her upper decks strewn with the dead and dying. Yet, she held out for almost an hour before she literally blew up, with her crewmen still manning the guns. Captain Kennedy, and all of his crew save eleven, lost their lives in that heroic action.

This was the first intimation that Worsley was to lead a charmed life. One time in the Mersey, *Laurentic* was prevented from docking by a terrible air raid on Liverpool, an all-night blitz which devastated large areas of town and harbour and wrecked many ships lying alongside. She lay helplessly at anchor out in the stream throughout a night made hideous by the roaring of fires and thunder of exploding bombs. Shattering blasts boomed all around the harbour, setting ships and buildings ablaze and toppling the giant dockside cranes. The city seemed to cower beneath a vast umbrella of smoke and lurid flames, and bombs which fell among the ships lying at anchor sent up huge waterspouts. But HMS *Laurentic* survived the nightmare, and on the following day she steamed slowly into the war-torn harbour to come alongside and dock.

*Laurentic's* massive old boilers were voracious consumers of coal, and when she needed to re-fill her bunkers, coaling took one whole day with the entire crew — including officers — required to lend a hand. It was a gruelling, filthy, back-breaking job. Several hundreds of tons of coal had to be humped up the gangway in sacks, with billowing clouds of gritty black dust clogging ears, eyes, nostrils and throats. Nevertheless, some members of the crew regarded this awful chore as a spot of light relief from a daily stint even more arduous.

These men, the stokers, fascinated Worsley. He swears that the notorious old Liverpool fireman was of a primeval breed apart, incredibly rough and twice as tough. With *Laurentic* rolling and pitching, buffeted by staggering seas, these men rushed big iron wheelbarrows piled high with coal along narrow gangways between the bunkers and an engine room

ARMED MERCHANT CRUISER HMS *LAURENTIC* 1942.
(Note the 6" shells in their 'ready use' deck racks.)

which resembled hell on earth. They worked near-naked, black with dust and streaming with sweat, in a clamorous inferno of heat and din. Any old seaman will testify that stokers on a coal-burning ship had the hardest, dirtiest and worst job in the world.

Small wonder, then, that once ashore these fellows got roaring drunk, and an inebriated Scouse fireman was a dangerous animal. He had an inbred hatred of Authority, and any human being with an officer's cap on his head was a target for instant violence. Any time that *Laurentic* had finished her coaling, and the firemen were returning off shore, was a time of trauma for Worsley and his messmates — Midshipmen Peter Nicholson age 19, and the brothers Mark and Rea Beadle. Unless off watch and safe in the mess, they ducked through hatches and scuttled along gangways to avoid coming face-to-face with some reeling, cursing fireman. This was not solely due to the fact that they wished to escape a fist to the head. In protecting themselves, the middies were also protecting the men, because although the Scouses were merchant seamen, Article T124 placed them under Royal Navy discipline and the punishment for striking an officer was swift and extremely severe.

After coaling HMS *Laurentic* would cast off and steam north. It is difficult now, and especially with regard to the ill-fated *Rawalpindi,* to view these lumbering old ships as anything other than sacrificial lambs. They were little more than floating targets for the very vessels they sought. All they could do was radio positions of sighted enemy ships, and hope to avoid a confrontation. Their obsolete six-inch guns were ludicrously slow to fire and re-load because shells and explosive charges were separate, man-handled into the breech from steel cradles stacked on the open deck. And yet, on one of her patrols, HMS *Laurentic* scored a day of triumph.

The Germans had armed some of their freighters in much the same way as an AMC was armed, but they hid their guns with canvas screens and steamed under neutral colours. On sighting one such vessel, Captain Vivian became suspicious in spite of the Swedish flag painted large on her side. He ordered her to heave to, took the German crew as prisoners, then sank the abandoned ship with gunfire. To quote John Worsley, it was 'splendid practise'.

Nevertheless, *Laurentic* was lucky. She survived one whole year of northern patrols without ever encountering a *Scharnhorst* or a *Gneisenau,* and these twelve months allowed young Worsley to 'learn as he went along'. It has often been said that any war, and especially war at sea, is 90 per cent boredom and 10 per cent terror. Assuming this to be true, *Laurentic*'s officers could be bored at their ease. Their ship had been a luxury liner, and they messed in its first class lounge, with all of its sumptuous furnishings. Anything less like the stark cramped quarters of a purpose-built warship would be difficult to imagine. They used the first class cabins, and slept in proper beds and so, when off-watch, were quite comfortable.

It was during these long cold vigils that Worsley began again to exercise his art, and many of his lively on-the-spot sketches depicting life on board appear in the pages of this book. The scenes evoke a vigour and vitality which only those drawn from life can ever succeed in capturing. Most of the original paintings and drawings are among the seventy-odd of his works now owned variously by the Maritime and Imperial War museums, whose curators were prompted to acquire them by that famous art historian, the late Lord (Kenneth) Clark.

'SMOKE ON THE HORIZON.'
Bridge activity at a sighting. Armed Merchant Cruiser HMS *Laurentic*, Northern Patrol 1940.

Various sailors at an ernest game! —
Study taken on the mess deck during a watch below.
The types of men are many and varied and infinitely rich in character.

HMS *LAURENTIC*.
Having been an Atlantic luxury liner pre-war, the *Laurentic* had big spacious mess decks.

Kenneth Clark had contrived at the outset of war to form a special committee whose task was to mount, at the National Gallery, a permanent exhibition of works by the various services' official war artists. John Worsley was not to be designated as such until July 1943, when he became the first of only two active-service sailors ever assigned that status. (He had, however, been commissioned in 1942 to illustrate John Fernald's book *Destroyer From America*.) In the meantime, Clark had recognised Worsley's earlier work as being the one and only source

depicting war at sea as it was actually happening, and he convinced his War Artists Advisory Committee that the sketches and paintings sent to him by Worsley deserved a special place in the permanent exhibition. Worsley continued to send his work to Kenneth Clark from wherever he was in the world, not excluding the confines of a German POW camp.

After surviving all of her patrols around Iceland, HMS *Laurentic* finally came to grief when taken out of those hazardous waters. After almost exactly one year of service in the North Atlantic, she was assigned to escort duty in a convoy bound for Gibraltar. She made the outward-bound passage unscathed, and almost made it back to base.

On 3 November 1940 she was steaming in company with another AMC, HMS *Petroclus*, and the ships were about 300 miles to the west of Northern Ireland. It was about nine o'clock on a cold murky night when Worsley, asleep in his bed, was rudely awakened by a terrific explosion and the strident clanging alarm which summoned all hands to action stations. In all that rush and frenzy there was another enormous boom as a second torpedo struck, and *Laurentic* began to heel. Up on deck, Worsley and the rest of his gun's crew could actually make out the shape of the German U-boat as it lay on the surface, but the ship was listing so badly they were unable to bring their guns to bear. Then, *Laurentic* reeled violently as she was torpedoed yet again, and the order was given to abandon ship.

The old liner did not sink immediately. Such an emergency had been foreseen, and all available space between decks had been filled with empty oil drums. These lent the ship a buoyancy which kept her afloat for twenty minutes or so. Time enough for Worsley, together with about thirty other survivors, to scramble down a rope ladder into a waterlogged cutter and they shivered in that wallowing shell, up to their waists in freezing water, throughout the hours of darkness. Pressed by the writer for an account of that grim winter night, Worsley's response was that it had been 'somewhat chilly'.

The cutter was sighted shortly after dawn by an old V&W* destroyer, and the rescued men were put ashore at Gourock on the River Clyde. There, they learned that their companion ship HMS *Petroclus* had also been sunk, presumably by the same U-boat.

This dual tragedy marked the beginning of the end for Britain's AMCs. It was patently reprehensible for the Chiefs of Staff to ask of any man that he risk his life in ships so vulnerable. Fifty-six had been requisitioned and by the summer of 1941, no fewer than 15 had been sent to the bottom. It was high time such ships were phased out.

*Known as such because their names all began with either 'V' or 'W'.

'RUM ISSUE.'
HMS *Laurentic*, Northern
Patrol, Atlantic 1940.

RUM ISSUE.

KING GOD BLESS

'DHOBI ON THE QUARTER
DECK.'

AN ABLE SEAMAN IN
*LAURENTIC*'S TRANSMITTING
STATION.

THE AFTER DECK (STARBOARD
SIDE) SEEN FROM THE
PROMENADE DECK

THE GERMAN VESSEL
DISGUISED WITH THE SWEDISH
FLAG ON HER SIDES WAS SUNK
AND HER CREW TAKEN
PRISONERS.

A GROUP OF WARSHIPS
ANCHORED IN THE CLYDE
OFF GREENOCK.

UNLOADING FISH FROM A
PASSING ICELANDIC TRAWLER
BARTERED FOR WITH RUM
AND TOBACCO.

*Unloading fish procured from a passing Trawler...*

*"Laurentic" 1940*

*John Worsley 1940*

Sta. 106/35.    "LANCASTER" 1941    312901r.  Wt.  30557/D.5886.  125m. pads.  10/39.  W. & S. Ld.  51-5091.

20

# CHAPTER 3
# ATLANTIC GALES

John Worsley was among the survivors from HMS *Laurentic* who were not left 'on the beach'. He had been seeking, whilst serving in the AMC, to be afforded proper RNVR status, and at last his request had been granted. From Gourock he was sent home on leave, with orders to report afterwards to HMS *King Alfred*, a Royal Navy shore establishment near Brighton. It was a most unusual procedure. Most volunteers had to complete their training *before* becoming naval officers: Worsley arrived at the shore establishment with the single wavy stripe of a RNVR sub-lieutenant already on his sleeve. Once again, the training was brief and intensive, with courses on gunnery, navigation, torpedoes, and ASDIC crammed into four short weeks. Armed with all this potted knowledge, Worsley joined his next ship.

HMS *Lancaster* — previously the USS *Philip* — was one of fifty World War One destroyers hastily taken out of mothballs and loaned or sold to Britain by the American government in the early days of the war. A splendid old four-stacker she was capable in ideal conditions of an astonishing 33 knots, but her narrow hull and round-bottomed construction so reduced her speed in rough seas as to make her incapable of keeping up with the convoys she was supposed to guard and protect.

Worsley joined HMS *Lancaster* at her base in the Kyle of Lochalsh, and was promptly assigned to the Ship's Office. He had undergone little enough training at best, but this was one duty about which he knew absolutely nothing, and within a couple of weeks he had 'lost' £25 from the Office's contingency fund! He would have liked to have taken advantage of his training on ASDICs (a method of detecting underwater objects such as mines and submarines by using high-frequency sound pulses, a kind of early Sonar) but relates ' . . . I was never allowed anywhere near!'

All of this aside, he was soon to learn that life on board a destroyer at sea was vastly different to his previous life in a converted luxury liner, and that Atlantic convoys' escort duty imposed a much more taxing regime. Each time HMS *Lancaster* steamed out of the Kyle of Lochalsh she was bound for three weeks of buffeting by the huge Atlantic seas with her crew working watch-and-watch: four hours 'on' followed by four hours 'off'. It was an extremely gruelling system, only sustainable by men who were young and fit. For three weeks on end they never had their clothes off, and were never able to sleep for longer than three hours at one time. After staggering below off watch they could only eat, or perhaps wash and shave, before falling into their bunks — or, in the case of men on the lower deck, climb wearily into their hammocks. It must have seemed to these crews that they barely had time to close their eyes before being called back on watch again.

After a full six months of this harsh routine, HMS *Lancaster* could withstand no more battering by the rough Atlantic gales. She was badly in need of a refit, and her captain received orders to steam all around the north coast of Scotland and down the east coast of England to Hull, there to put his ship in dry dock. The fact that these orders came none too soon is manifest in a grimly-humorous story which Worsley tells with evident relish.

Those were the days when every civilian dockyard foreman affected the same curious 'uniform' of drab tan raincoat and bowler hat, and invariably carried a sort of staff of office in the form of a rolled umbrella which he used for prodding and poking. With *Lancaster* propped up in her dry basin, one such fellow inspected her exposed bottom in the time-honoured manner and was awestruck to find some plates so corroded that the tip of his brolly went straight through! It was patently obvious that the old destroyer would not be made seaworthy in fewer than seven or eight weeks, and her crew was not to be left idle in the meantime.

Worsley was posted forthwith to join HMS *Wallace*, another old V&W destroyer and the leader of a convoys' escort group operating between Rosyth and Sheerness, up and down the notorious 'E-boat Alley'. This was one area of operations at sea wherein the proverbial ratio of '90 per cent boredom and 10 per cent terror' was most definitely reversed. After the fall of France, Germany took control of the Channel ports and used them as very convenient bases for both surface and undersea marauders. The surface E-boats were small, fast craft purpose-built for the firing of torpedoes, and were equipped with extremely powerful engines. They infested the Channel and the east coast waters, and most of their attacks were made with inpunity. A great many Allied vessels were sunk, and not a few of them warships. The terrible ravages in E-boat Alley became so commonplace that hardly a single convoy passed through these waters unscathed. Losses were constant, and heavy.

As with ASDIC, these were the early days of radar, and east coast convoys plotted their courses on a long succession of buoys anchored at intervals to mark the passage. The Germans, quick to detect this system, adopted a practise of mooring their E-boats to those very same buoys, because the Allies' primitive radar screens were incapable of showing the difference between an unattended buoy and one which was nursing a parasite. For the E-boat skipper, nothing could have been easier. All he had to do was sneak out of harbour at dead of night, make fast to one of the buoys, and simply wait for his prey to come to him.

Another traumatic aspect of those east coast convoys was one which concerned the RAF. Royal Air Force bombers flying low towards home after raids on Germany were frequently met with a barrage of anti-aircraft fire from the guns of our own ships, and sometimes even shot down.

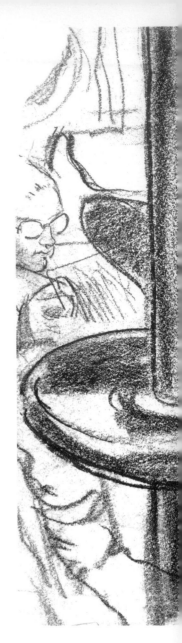

'HMS *Lancaster.*'
Off watch in the wardroom.

Again, it was a problem of identification. Just as ship's radar was incapable of distinguishing whether or not a buoy was attended by an E-boat there was no possible way, at night, that ships' anti-aircraft batteries could ever be quite sure that aeroplanes on a low approach were not those of the enemy. When in doubt, shoot first, because there might be no second chance.

The very proper fury of RAF personnel was only partly allayed by the carrying on board ship of RAF observers and inviting them, in the dark and under stress, to make fast and accurate decisions as to whether or not this or that approaching aircraft was 'one of ours' or 'one of theirs'. The RAF men were compelled to admit failure, and the dilemma was partly resolved by issuing bomber pilots with orders to maintain as much height as possible until actually coming in to land.

Worsley's spell of duty in E-boat Alley lasted only two months but HMS *Wallace,* as convoy leader, was always in the van, and he describes the experience as 'somewhat hairy'.

HMS *WALLACE*.
Gun crew fuse setters at work.

ICE FLOES OFF GREENLAND, NORTHERN PATROL, 1940.
Looking over the forecastle of the Armed Merchant Cruiser HMS *Laurentic*.

THE SINKING OF HMS *LAURENTIC*, 3 NOVEMBER, 1940.
180 miles west of Galway. Position 54.09 N. 13.44 W. at 22.51. Sunk by three torpedos from U99 Kapitan Otto Kretschmer. Losses approximately 100. A Canadian Sub Lieutenant was last off, watched by us in the water as he clambered up the steepening forecastle with a torch, and as the ship disappeared he was left floating, belieing the belief that a sinking ship will always suck everything down with it. (*Imperial War Museum*)

'LINE AHEAD.'
Stern wash from the destroyer HMS *Lancaster*.

INDIAN OCEAN TROOP CONVOY FROM ADEN TO FREMANTLE, 1942.
Left to right: HMS *Devonshire*, MS *New Amsterdam*, MS *Aquitania*, MS *Queen Mary*, MS *Isle de France*. 'Walrus' flying boat spotter 'plane from HMS *Devonshire* in the air.

MALTA GRAND HARBOUR EARLY SUMMER, 1943.
Middle foreground is the battleship HMS *Nelson*, astern of her HMS *Repulse*, left the Monitor HMS *Roberts* from which the Salerno bombarding and smoke screen pictures were made. (*Imperial War Museum*)

INFANTRY LANDING CRAFT (LCIs) ENTERING CATANIA, SICILY, AUGUST, 1943.
Mount Etna in the background showing on the slopes the British lines left and the Germans right with artillery explosions and fighting still going on. (*Imperial War Museum*)

East Coast 41

H.M.S. "Wallace"
East coast convoy 1941

HMS *Wallace*, East coast convoy, 1941.

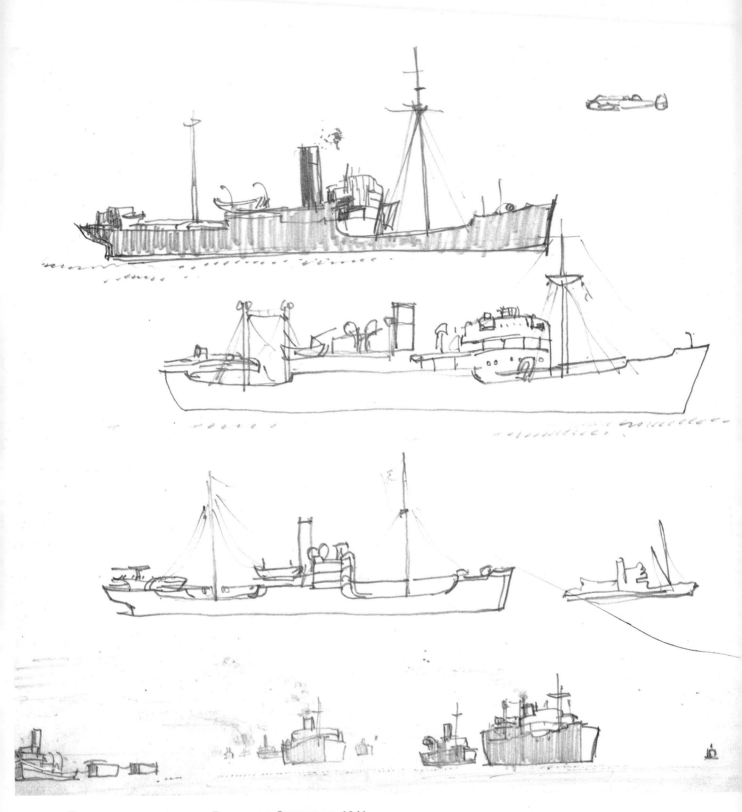

EAST COAST CONVOY SHIPS, ROSYTH TO SHEERNESS, 1941

'IN THE TAILOR'S SHOP.'
HMS *Ranpura*, Christmas, 1941.

In the Taylors shop.

# CHAPTER 4
# FAR EASTERN WATERS

Immediately following his short spell of running the gauntlet in E-boat Alley, Worsley was posted to his second AMC, but his service in HMS *Ranpura* was even shorter than that in HMS *Wallace*. After an uneventful passage across the Atlantic and up into Chesapeake Bay, he was ordered to proceed from Baltimore (which he did by pleasure boat!) back down the bay to the premier U.S. naval base at Norfolk, Virginia. There, he was to join the big 'County' class cruiser HMS *Devonshire*, assigned to duty in the far east as escort to the troopship convoys steaming across the Indian Ocean between Aden and Australia.

HMS *Devonshire* left Norfolk late in the Spring of 1942, bound first for Freetown in Sierra Leone on the west coast of Africa. After refuelling there, she steamed south to Cape Town, where her crew was given a few days leave. Oddly — because Cape Town is a spectacular landfall, and he made the usual sightseeing trips, including one to the top of the mount Table Mountain — Worsley made only one painting during this visit. Perhaps there was only time enough to relax and enjoy himself before *Devonshire* left to traverse the Cape bound for Durban, her next port of call.

Initially, *Devonshire* was to have adopted Durban as her base of operations. In the event, she did not, a decision which might possibly have been influenced by the fact that certain elements of the black population were giving rise to concern. Sailors of HM ships presented a target for these ethnical dissidents and were warned before stepping ashore that after the hours of darkness, they had better stay on the alert.

The officer's club in Durban was about a mile and a half from where *Devonshire* lay alongside, and once when Worsley left the premises alone and late at night he began to feel apprehensive. He picked up a good-sized brick and carried it, as a weapon of self-defence, until he was safely back on board. He recalls the incident somewhat shame-facedly but the writer, having more than once come close to falling victim to racial hatred violence in South Africa, can heartily endorse his prudence.

HMS *Devonshire* steamed out of Durban with Mombasa as her next port of call before heading further north to Aden, where she picked up the first of her many troopship convoys. These convoys were not especially large in numbers of ships, but the ships themselves were big. They included such giants as the old *Queen Mary, Aquatania, Ile de France,* and *New Amsterdam.* Carrying a total of many thousands of troops these mighty vessels made very fast passages averaging around 24 knots, and they needed to be heavily guarded.

Having regard to the sheer size of the ships, and the speed at which they steamed, the task of maintaining a tight station was by no means easy even in the full light of day. At night, with the ships blacked out, it was an extremely tense operation. The convoys pursued a zig-zag course, veering in unison like a well-trained troop of formation dancers, and one slight mistake could result in disaster. In sea lanes more restricted than those of the Indian Ocean collisions were by no means uncommon, and even in that vast expanse of blue water there were some very narrow escapes. One such extremely close encounter, and this between heavy warships, is described by John Worsley as ' . . . the most frightening experience of my life'.

He was on the bridge in the black of night, keeping the middle watch (midnight to four am) when the change of course became due. He was conscious as he gave the order that HMS *Repulse* was on a parallel course, slightly ahead and to starboard. *Devonshire*'s cox'n obeyed the instruction, and her great bows began to come round. As he strove to peer through the darkness, Worsley's mouth went abruptly dry. He could just make out the pale boiling turbulence of *Repulse*'s massive wake. One of the two great warships had made a 'zig' when she ought to have made a 'zag', and they appeared to be heading for an almighty collision. Horrified, Worsley yelled for hard a'starboard and then held his breath, waiting for the rending crunch which mercifully never came. In those terrible few minutes of fearful suspense, two ships passed in the night as closely as two ships ever passed, and Worsley breathed a huge sigh of relief. It took him the whole of the remainder of his watch to come back on course and set *Devonshire* safely back on station, and not least to get over his shock. He did not log the incident and fortunately for him, the Officer of the Watch in *Repulse* appeared to remain in ignorance of her dangerously narrow escape, because Worsley heard no more of the incident. What the cox'n thought will always remain a matter for speculation.

In the meantime, however, Worsley saw some lively action when HMS *Devonshire* was ordered to join a task force assembling at Durban under the command of Rear-Admiral E. N. Syfret for an assault on Madagascar. The Royal Navy had no safe base between Simonstown on the Cape and Kilindini at Mombasa, and this long gap in the protection of vital convoys steaming from the Cape up to Egypt was a potentially hazardous one. The operation was necessary because Madagascar was held by French forces of the Vichy government, which was collaborating with Germany and so with the Axis. The ground assault force together with its supplies and equipment left England in March 1942 and steamed 8,000 miles to rendezvous at Durban with a powerful fleet of warships drawn from home waters, Force H. at Gibraltar, and the Far Eastern squadrons.

Admiral Syfret's main objective was to take and secure the splendid well-fortified harbour at Diego Suarez, on Madagascar's west coast.

The attack was launched in the very early hours of the morning of 5

OPPOSITE

'CHRISTMAS DAY IN THE GALLEY.'
HMS *Ranpura*, 1941.

Christmas day in
the galley!

HMS *DEVONSHIRE*, 1942.
Off duty on the mess deck.

May 1942, with *Devonshire* lending full weight to the thunderous barrage
with salvoes from her big eight-inchers. Under a night sky made brilliant
by enormous flashes from the warships' heavy guns, and whilst sweepers
went in under the barrage to clear the harbour approaches of mines,
bombers and fighters from the aircraft carriers *Indomitable* and *Illustrious*
flew in overhead to neutralise the airfields held by the French. A
detachment of fifty Royal Marines from HMS *Devonshire* was transferred,
along with 'bootnecks' from other big ships, to a destroyer which was to
take them in and land them ashore. The Vichy French forces put up stiff
resistance, but the destroyer penetrated their defences and forced its way
into the harbour actually to come alongside and deposit the Marines on a

dock. *Devonshire*'s main contribution to this successful operation was to wipe out with accurate gunfire a battery of searchlights which had fixed the destroyer in their glare. The expedition was a total success, and after carrying out their mission every one of *Devonshire*'s fighting Marines made his way back on board to resume his mundane shipboard duties. Madagascar was finally secured around noon on 7 May, and Admiral Syfret took the main body of his fleet into the now-safe harbour of Diego Suarez on the evening of that day.

HMS *Devonshire* was returned to her escort duties and reached Fremantle in Australia towards the very end of June, and it was there that Worsley enjoyed a less-harrowing experience. Following the Japanese attack on Pearl Harbor on 7 December 1941 the U.S. Navy had established a submarine base at Fremantle and the cruiser's officers knowing that all U.S. ships and shore bases were 'dry', conceived the gesture of inviting their American allies to a drinks party on board ship. The party was a great success, and *Devonshire*'s captain received a visit on the morning after from the commander of the submarine fleet. After expressing his thanks for the splendid hospitality afforded his men, he went on to say what a pity it was that the jollifications had not coincided with America's greatest national holiday, Independence Day. His British counterpart was quick to take the hint, and the party he authorised for the fourth of July was even bigger and better than the previous one. It is interesting to speculate how many of the roistering Americans paused to consider the irony of a situation wherein the open-handed hosts of their revelries were representatives of that very nation whose rejection, in 1776, they were so joyously celebrating!

Half a world away from German U-boats and E-boats, and with the Japanese navy kept hotly occupied by the fighting ships of U.S. Admiral Chester Nimitz, those far eastern convoys of 1942/43 were almost entirely free from attack. *Devonshire*'s lumbering Walrus seaplane, launched from its catapult amidships, carried out regular reconnaissance flights and returned with no danger to report. Off watch, the ship's company were able to relax, and sunbathe under the guns. There was leisure for reading, and the writing of letters. Worsley spent much of his free time with palette and pencil, making an accurate pictorial record of his year in *Devonshire*.

But having been promoted to full lieutenant, his duties during this haitus of '90 per cent boredom' had become rather more diverse. He was now a Divisional Officer, responsible for the discipline and well-being of a section of the ship's crew, with authority to dole out minor punishments. This last posed no great problem as offences were fairly rare and in any case, penalties for offences were broadly defined in the 'seamen's bible,' or K.Rs. & A.Is. (*King's Regulations and Admiralty Instructions*). Much more perturbing to him was the fact that at 22 years old, and with little real experience of the human condition, he was called upon to render advice and solace to men some of whom were years older than himself.

The most common request for his counsel came from sailors who were worried about their wives. The ubiquitous 'well-meaning' friend or neighbour would drop a line to Jack, often as not anonymously, to appraise him of some marital infidelity going on behind his back, causing Jack to seek the 'fatherly' advice of his divisional officer. As often as the problem arose, Worsley never knew quite what to say. Mail to and from home took about three weeks each way and he knew that most probably, in the meantime, Jolly Jack would run ashore in Bombay or Colombo hell-bent on perpertrating that same naughtiness of which his wife was accused.

Second only to Colombo in Ceylon, Bombay was a favourite port of call. It had (and still has) a distinctive aroma all of its very own. It smells like no other city on earth, a curiously pungent, spicy odour so powerful and all-pervasive it assails the nostrils of those on board ship whilst still several miles off shore. But in spite of much filth and abject poverty the city teemed with a life which, to Jack, was exotic and exciting. Being a lover of curries, Worsley vastly enjoyed the huge variety of food.

Metaphorically, and in every way, Colombo was a different kettle of fish. Ex-patriate Britishers there, alerted to the arrival of a convoy of H.M. ships, would line the docks with their motor cars and issue invitations all round for the crews to join their families 'up homers' for a day or two of rest in congenial surroundings before putting back to sea. (This benefice was not peculiar to Ceylon; it was offered, too, in South African ports and in those of Australia. These people, enormously kind, proliferated in many parts of the world and they made an important contribution to the maintenance of morale.)

One such warm-hearted benefactor was 'Coco' Craib, a wealthy tea planter with a large estate in the hills behind the port. It was Worsley's good fortune to fall in with Craib and to become his regular guest. Whenever *Devonshire* came alongside at Colombo old Coco would be there in his Rolls-Royce waiting to drive Worsley to his splendid house built high on the crest of a hill with magnificent views on every side. To visit the house was to experience real luxury. Craib had made a lot of money out of tea, and the place was sumptuously furnished in the very best of taste. Nothing was too good for Craib's Royal Navy guests. They ate and drank like emperors, and were given the run of his entire estate. He was a hugely generous host.

He was also an eccentric old buffer, very fond of practical jokes. He had a favourite pet mynah bird which he had trained to perform amusing tricks and to mimic its master's voice to perfection. With Craib and his guests lounging in planter's chairs on the verandah the bird would suddenly shout 'BOY!', and one of the servants would hurry out to freshen up the drinks.

Worsley recalls one of the many jokes which Coco Craib played on him. They were seated about to start dinner, and among the mass of silver which decorated the long table were two large covered soup tureens. Coco asked Worsley which he preferred, mulligatawny soup, or cream of pea. Worsley said he had no special preference, and would take the one nearest to his end of the table. He was invited to help himself. When he lifted the lid he almost fell off his chair as a vicious-looking snake reared its head. When Coco had managed to stop laughing he apologised for causing the scare, and pushed across the second tureen. This time when Worsley lifted the lid a frantic bird shot out and flapped around the room with squawks of outrage.

Worsley soon learned to stop admiring the many *objets d'art* which graced the bungalow, because to admire a piece was to have it given. This applied to objects both large and small, even to furniture. 'Take it, dear boy, it's yours. Take it home!' And at the end of every day, Craib would invite his guest to choose anything in the house, anything at all, and keep it for his own. Worsley had so many gifts pressed upon him it would have taken a small freighter to ship them all back to UK. All were accepted with dignity, but the only thing Worsley actually brought home was the memory of a most unusual man.

After one whole year of steaming to and fro across the Indian Ocean, HMS *Devonshire* was ordered back to the UK for a refit. She paid off at Newcastle-on-Tyne in the summer of 1943, and for Worsley it marked the end of an era. His war had a long way to go, but he was about to embark upon a new beginning.

FOUR SAILORS, HMS *DEVONSHIRE*, 1942.

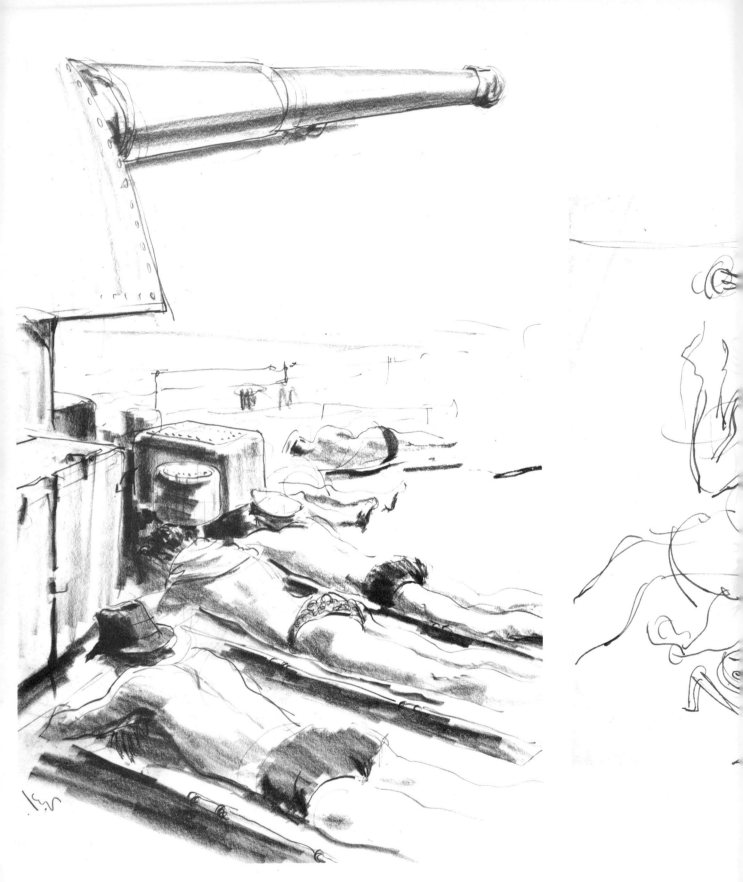

HMS DEVONSHIRE.
Officers sunbathing on the quarter deck under 'Y' turret 8" guns.

HMS *DEVONSHIRE.*
Lookouts in the Indian Ocean.

*DEVONSHIRE*'S WALRUS SEAPLANE MOUNTED ON ITS CATAPULT.

AFTER A FLIGHT THE WALRUS HAD TO BE HOISTED BACK ON BOARD.

*Hoisting in the 'Walrus'*
*HMS 'Devonshire' 1942*

Kilindini

AFTER MAST, HMS *DEVONSHIRE*.

42

*our 1942*

KILINDINI HARBOUR, MOMBASA.
'D' class cruiser in the foreground.

'LEADING SEAMAN.'

H.M.S. "NEWFOUNDLAND" stern blown off by a mine

John Worsley
Malta 1943

46

# CHAPTER 5
# INTO THE LION'S MOUTH

Just as Worsley had become a man of the sea, there was now no doubt in the mind of Kenneth Clark that he was also an important artist whose work was quite unique. His were the only drawings and paintings actually to depict war at sea, executed on the spot, and they remain today as the only significant source of such material. So, with Kenneth Clark as his champion, the War Artists Advisory Committee voted in July 1943 to elect John Worsley as the first of only two active-service naval War Artists appointed during World War Two.

Worsley knew nothing of this, and spent his last few days in HMS *Devonshire* making paintings of her refitting, one of which evokes a dramatic little story. The boy depicted in the foreground was a happy little chap, always busy bustling about. Even as Worsley was painting this scene on the forecastle, the boy slipped and fell on the greasy deck and with a sudden yell of alarm disappeared head-first into the hawse-hole. A horrified Worsley rushed below and stumbled down a long succession of ladders to the chain locker, and after wrenching open the hatch found to his vast relief that the boy, although badly bruised and shaken, had come to no serious harm. Dockyard workers had left a heap of sacks on top of the huge iron links of the cable, and these had cushioned his fall.

When *Devonshire* had completed her paying-off, Worsley expected to be posted to another ship. Instead, he received orders to report to the Admiralty for an interview with Admiral Sir William James. He did so somewhat fearfully, wondering what it was all about: a lowly lieutenant in the RNVR summoned to appear before one of the highest-ranking officers in His Majesty's senior service. Like many another sailor, he asked himself what chickens he might have hatched which had not (yet) come home to roost? Could it be that very near-miss with *Repulse*?

His qualms were soon dismissed. Admiral James — who was the model, in his childhood for the famous 'Bubbles' portrait used by Pears Soap in an advertising campaign — received him graciously in a beautiful room at the Admiralty. Then, standing with his back to the fire, he appraised the young lieutenant of his new appointment and instructed him how he must proceed. 'My boy, you are the youngest Official War Artist ever. You will join the Staff of the Commander-in-Chief, Mediterranean, but I don't want you sitting on your backside in Malta. Get out, and go where the action is. Get into the lion's mouth.'

Little did Worsley know, then, where the admiral's order was fated to lead him. He was told to present himself at Northolt aerodrome, out of uniform, for a flight across neutral Spain. The flight was made at night, in a stripped-down Liberator bomber. He had three fellow-passengers, all of whom wore civilian clothes, a trio of Frenchmen with hardly a word of English between them. When next morning the Liberator landed at Fez in Morocco and all four, including Worsley, changed into uniform, the latter was abashed by their splendour. He found he had been travelling in company with three full Generals of the Free French Army. He never learned the object of their mission, or what became of them. The next leg of his long journey was made in a Dakota, and being the only passenger, he sat up front in the cockpit beside the pilot. They flew across the desert in daytime, and he was much impressed by the amazing scene spread out below. The desert sands were one vast maze of tanktracks and littered with abandoned armour, the detritus of huge battles fought over countless miles.

He spent two days in Tunis waiting for a flight to Malta before being told that an aircraft, another Dakota, would be leaving that afternoon. Arriving at the airstrip at the appointed time, he and the pilot had to hang around waiting for a second passenger who turned up almost one hour late. Worsley remembers this character as the most boorish and unsociable man he ever came across. He merely grunted in reply to Worsley's greeting, sat as far away as he could, and never spoke a word throughout the two and a half hours in the air. When the Dakota finally landed at Malta he was whisked away in a car with not a word of goodbye, and Worsley never saw the fellow again. His name was Randolph Churchill.

Worsley was met at Malta by Lt. Guy Morgan, a man who quickly became his friend and one with whom he was later to share a remarkable adventure. But that was for the future, and he busied himself in the meantime making paintings and sketches. The ancient and massive Grand Harbour at Valletta, torn and ravaged by numerous heavy bombing raids, presented an amazing spectacle. Its wet and dry docks were crammed with warships, many of them heavily damaged and swarming with workmen toiling around the clock on repairs. One of these, the cruiser HMS *Newfoundland*, subject of a fine drawing by Worsley now in the Imperial War Museum, had survived to limp into harbour with the whole of her stern blown off.

Lt. Guy Morgan, ex-*Daily Express* journalist, whose duty in Malta was that of R.N. Liaison Officer for newspaper war correspondents, was a man of considerable stature. Some of his war correspondent charges were made of stuff less stern and one of these, the man from the *Daily Mirror*, disgraced himself rather badly. Assigned to a tour of duty aboard a minesweeper, he spent an entire week up on deck, refusing ever to go below for fear of being trapped there should the sweeper strike one of those very dangerous objects she was clearing from the sea. Worse, he nagged at the crew, reminding them what a terribly hazardous job they were doing, and beseeching them to take great care. Infuriated by this constant sedition, and its resultant wearing-down of morale, the skipper

PART OF THE INVASION FLEET SAILING FROM BIZERTA TO SALERNO.
Code named 'Avalaunch', September 8, 1943. HMS *Roberts* the monitor in the centre distance.

HMS *ROBERTS* MAKING SMOKE TO HIDE LANDING SHIPS TRANSPORT (LSTs) FROM
GERMAN ARTILLERY. SALERNO, SEPTEMBER 9, 1943.

THE MONITOR HMS *ROBERTS* BOMBARDING WITH HER 15" GUNS AT THE SALERNO
LANDING, SEPTEMBER 10, 1943.
Small Infantry Landing Craft (LCIs) coming in under the fire.

WRECKED MOTOR BOAT, GRAND HARBOUR, MALTA, 1943.

put back into Valletta and set the fellow ashore. Fortunately, the man
from the *Mirror* was not at all typical of his colleagues, most of whom
were brave men.

Worsley's first real venture into the lion's mouth was made in an LCI
(Landing Craft, Infantry) loaded with troops and supplies bound for
Catania to reinforce the invasion of Sicily. It was very soon after the initial
assault, and with Axis forces still massed in the north, there was still much
heavy fighting. British naval forces for the invasion, code-named
Operation Husky, were under the overall command of Admiral Sir
Andrew Cunningham, with Admiral Sir Bertram Ramsey responsible for
the first direct attack on the eastern seaboard. The attack by American
forces in the areas of Licata and Gela on the western coast was
commanded by Vice-Admiral H. K. Hewitt, USN, and the first
bombardments opened up shortly before dawn on the morning of 10 July
1943.

The port of Catania lies under the towering massif of Mount Etna,
and the battle which raged as Worsley's LCI approached the harbour
seemed almost to be for possession of the volcano itself rather than for the
town at the foot of its slopes. British forces had occupied the harbour, but
possession was still being hotly disputed by Axis forces entrenched to the
north exchanging heavy artillery fire with the Allied armies advancing

from the south. Opposition to Admiral Ramsey's force came in the main from air and submarine attacks. The latter inflicted less damage than did the former, and during the first three weeks of the assault on Sicily eight Italian and three German submarines were sunk and another, the Italian *Bronzo,* blown to the surface and captured. The island was finally cleared of Axis resistance around the middle of August.

But this is Worsley's story, and after making action pictures of the fighting around Catania he visited Augusta and Syracuse down the coast to the south. The harbour at Augusta was littered with the wreckage of Italian float-planes, and although now secured by Allied forces, the port remained under attack from the air. Worsley continued to make drawings and paintings of the scene, including several of the enormous, cathedral-like rock caverns at Augusta (known as the Meilili Caves) used by the Germans as engineering workshops and for the storage of ammunitions and mines.

After a short respite back in Malta during which he sorted out and put finishing touches to the drawings and paintings he had made in Sicily, Worsley received permission from the C-in-C to accompany the forces then forming up for a big assault on the Italian mainland. There was considerable disagreement between the Allied Chiefs of Staff as to precisely when the main landings should be attempted, but it was finally agreed that D-day should be 9 September, with the big main thrust being concentrated on forming beach-heads around the bay of Salerno. In the meantime, however, there was to be a preliminary landing at Reggio, just across the Straits of Messina from Northern Sicily, where it was known there would be only small resistance. Privileged to witness the action from any vessel of his choosing, Worsley elected to do so in a Flack Landing Craft. These small ships were designed to accompany assault forces and lay off close inshore in order to provide anti-aircraft cover with their 'pom-pom' guns. He had decided that the bridge of an FLC was the ideal platform from which to record the assault.

The theory was sound, but the practicalities were rather different. In the black of night which preceded the dawn of the morning of 3 September, he set up his easel and prepared his palette all ready for the moment when there would be light enough to see and record the landings. He was up on the FLC's bridge, directly between the pom-

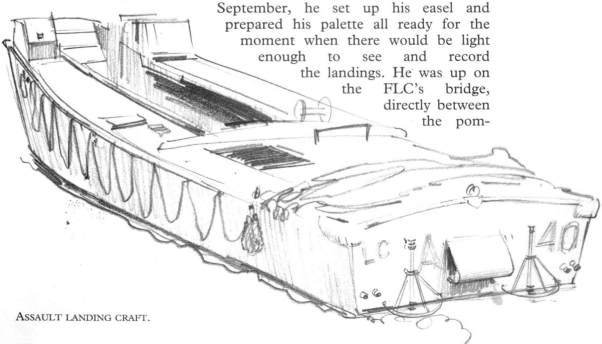

ASSAULT LANDING CRAFT.

poms mountings. As the sun began to rise above the horizon he was ready with brushes in hand. The thunderous attack began as the earliest gleams streaked the sky, but the dawning light brought fierce resistance from fighters and bombers of the Italian Air Force. He had scarcely begun to paint when ack-ack fire from the FLC's pom-poms on either side of him sent everything — easel, paints, and himself and all — flying in different directions. The experience came as a shock, and Worsley now admits in hindsight to a curious psychological block: having been appointed as an official war artist he had somehow considered himself immune from the dangers of actual combat. A sort of neutral observer, non-combative, and therefore in an abstract position somewhere 'outside' the conflict. His rude awakening came on that morning, and he never again attempted to make paintings under fire. Instead, he made numerous pencil sketches on a hand-held drawing board, as references for future paintings in conditions rather less fraught.

Six days after Reggio, the attack on Salerno was launched, and this time Worsley took ship in HMS *Roberts,* a monitor. Monitors, much bigger than FLCs, were designed to do much the same sort of job albeit on a grander scale. Whereas FLCs accompanied invasion forces, monitors went in ahead of them to soften up resistance by bombardment, and only then to lay off shore as protection against attack from the air. *Roberts* steamed out of Bizerta harbour on the afternoon of 7 September to rendezvous with a fleet which included two battleships, two aircraft carriers, four cruisers, and seventeen destroyers. The big main body of this naval covering force, under the command of Vice-Admiral Willis, left Malta's Grand Harbour and passed to the west of Sicily into the Tyrrhenian Sea before heading north-west for the Gulf of Salerno. The fleet was attacked by German and Italian torpedo-bombers during the night of 8–9 September, but all ships survived to take up their stations off the landing beaches in Salerno Bay in time to provide cover for the assault forces. The enemy defences were strong, and in spite of tremendous ship-to-shore bombardment and continuous attack by 'planes from the two British aircraft carriers, the invasion was met with fierce resistance. As the landing craft approached they came under heavy fire from the German shore emplacements, and those troops who survived to wade ashore found themselves engaged in bitter contest for possession of the beaches. Nevertheless, the British Army forces under General Montgomery had secured the beach-heads by nightfall, although the struggle to move forward inland was to rage for more than a week.

Worsley was given what he calls a dress-circle seat high up in the director tower of HMS *Roberts* from which to view the performance, and made many pictures during the first four days of the fighting before taking ship in a minesweeper for a passage back to Malta through the Straits of Messina. This was, if anything, even more traumatic an experience than the actual invasion itself. The sweeper's small crew had had little or no rest since the start of the invasion, and every man was half-asleep on his feet, but the ever-present threat of attack still remained. Four lookouts posted on the wings of the bridge, two on the port side and two on the starboard, were supplemented by Worsley and the Captain amidships, and the cox'n at the wheel. The Captain and Worsley spied an object floating in the sea ahead. As they drew closer, it proved to be the body of a German airman. None of the nodding seamen spotted the body until it was drifting past alongside, and one of the starboard lookouts snapped

THESE SKETCHES SHOW DIFFERENT CAMOUFLAGES IN USE DURING THIS PERIOD.

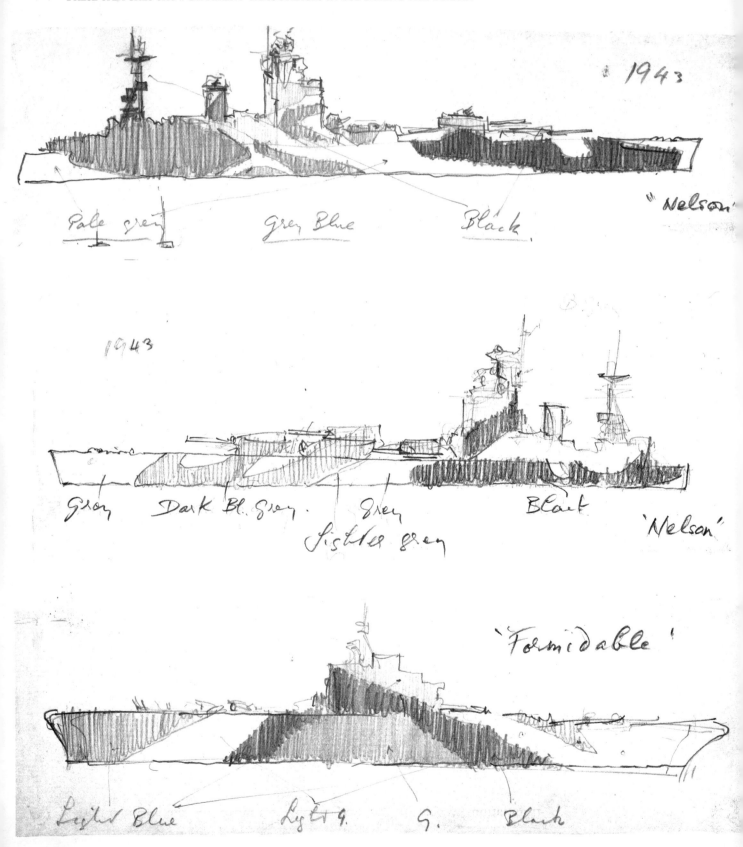

1943

"Nelson"

Pale grey        Grey Blue        Black

1943

'Nelson'

Grey    Dark Bl. grey.    Grey      Black
         Lighter grey

'Formidable'

Light Blue     Light g.     G.     Black

out of an involuntary doze. But instead of making an immediate report he nudged his oppo awake, and nodding down at the floating corpse remarked with typical grim wartime humour, 'Look at that bugger. I'll bet he's had more bloody sleep than we 'ave in these last four days!'

Back in Malta, Worsley occupied his time during what he dismisses as a 'bit of a rest' carving an Epsteinesque sculpture from a block of Maltese stone. This otherwise unimportant item of work is worthy of special mention because after he was captured by the Germans, the figure was carefully crated and freighted back to England and delivered to his home. It stands now in the garden which adjoins his studio, a constant reminder of those long-gone days, and a monument to the scrupulous care with which the Admiralty looked after a missing man's possessions.

Very soon, though, Worsley was back on the job assigned to him by Admiral 'Bubbles' James, and was steaming up to Tarranto, inside the heel of Italy. The Italian government had capitulated within a fortnight of the Salerno landings and by this time the Allied invasion forces had advanced considerably to the north. Seeking to see just how far he could get to the front-line fighting, Worsley hitched a ride across the heel of Italy to Bari on the east coast. He was given a lift by Lt. Ritchie (now retired Admiral Ritchie) a naval hydrographer, which further serves to illustrate the many facets of active service operative during that war. Moving on from Bari, Worsley the sailor proceeded north overland to the still-beleaguered port of Termoli, and it was here that he met an extraordinary character in the person of army Major Brian Robb. Robb, a Scotsman, had previously been a fashion artist employed by the *Daily Express*. Now, he was in charge of a band of native guerillas whose task was to infiltrate areas behind the German lines and cause havoc by sabotage.

A travel-stained John Worsley first met Major Robb in the pig-stye basement of an Italian farmhouse, and it was an encounter he can never forget. He interrupted a game of poker played in gloomy candle-light between Robb and a group of ruffian-like partisans. Robb looked up from his hand of cards and said ' . . . And *what* can we do for *you*?' It was a most bizarre encounter, like a dramatic scene from a film. Worsley told Robb what he wanted, and Robb did his best to oblige. He made it possible for Worsley to ship in an MTB (Motor Torpedo Boat) on a number of forays to the north of Termoli, the object being to put agents and saboteurs ashore behind the enemy lines.

It must be remembered that Worsley, although an official war artist, was also on active service and so expected to 'pull his weight' as a sailor whenever necessary. So it was that on one of these clandestine operations, the skipper of the MTB asked him to lend a hand. A small group of native partisans one of whom was a priest — or, at least, was dressed as a priest — was to be put ashore at intervals up the coast to the north. As usual, the skipper had chosen a moonless night, pitch-dark and very still, and as the MTB crept into a little bay at Chioggia all on board could hear the rumbling of German tanks and transports moving along the coast road. MTBs had large noisy engines even when idling, and as the skipper eased his boat as close to the beach as he dared, Worsley felt sure that those on shore *must* hear the racket it made. His own part in this particular operation was to ferry the priest ashore, which he did with great trepidation. When the rubber dinghy grounded on the sand and the priest, encumbered by a belt of hand grenades hidden under his cassock,

jumped ashore, Worsley breathed a sigh of relief. Then, as he began to pull back to the MTB, his passenger cried *'Momento! Momento! My bicycle, I must have my bicycle!'* So with sounds of German troop movements still in his ears, and expecting at any moment to hear the opening-up of machine gun fire, Worsley rowed back to the MTB, collected the bicycle, and made the hazardous trip all over again.

As has already been indicated, these clandestine operations of Worsley's were not solely confined to the infiltrating of partisan guerillas. Allied secret service agents were also put ashore. At that time — late September 1943 — the Italians, having surrendered, released their British prisoners of war. Unfortunately, some 2,000 of these were set free in territory well to the north of the Allied advance, and many of them were hiding in the Apennine Mountains, living extremely rough. They were never sure as to whether or not they could rely on co-operation and help from the local populace, and their situation was desperate. Somehow, and soon, they *had* to be helped and the man put in charge of helping them was Lt. Anthony Bentley-Buckle, RN. Major Robb introduced Lt. Worsley to Lt. Bentley-Buckle, and so it came about that Worsley spent most of the rest of his war in a German prison camp.

OPPOSITE
MELLILI CAVES, FORT AUGUSTA, SICILY.
These were natural caves additionally excavated by the Germans in which they had workshops and mine stores. Note that 'jolly Jack' has chalked a face on the nearest mine.

Mines stored in Melilli ... ... Sicily
... 465 were fo... ...

55

M.T. Driver. on
passage by air between
Algiers + Tunis
Aug 4 /43

Weiblicher Fahrer
LKW!

AMERICAN MT DRIVER IN DAKOTA ON PASSAGE BETWEEN ALGIERS AND TUNIS.
This was drawn before capture and note the German caption added later.

LANDING AT REGGIO ACROSS THE STRAITS OF MESSINA, 3 SEPTEMBER, 1943.
Landing Ships Transport landing guns and vehicles on the beaches with DUKWS following in astern.

L.S.Ts landing guns and vehicles at Reggio Italy. 3 Sept 43 with "Dukws" coming in astern.    John Worsley 43

Reggio beach 4 Sept '43   L.C.M. Landing tra

REGGIO BEACH.

REINFORCEMENTS EMBARKING AT SANTA TERESA DI RIVO, SICILY, BEFORE CROSSING TO REGGIO.

Sept 4 1943 reinforcements embarking at

'Dukws' leaving the water landing in Italy.

'DUKWS' COMING ASHORE.

Teresa di Rivo, Sicily, before crossing to Reggio

43 Reggio

ON THE BRIDGE OF A MINESWEEPER RETURNING THROUGH THE STRAITS OF MESSINA FROM THE SALERNO LANDING.
The sailor in the small dark box to the left of the picture is the Asdic (Anti-Submarine Detector) operator.

Brian Robb of
the Daily Express.

John Worsley
Oct 1943.

Italian agents
and saboteurs in
M.T.B. on the way
to be landed at Chioggia
Adriatic

ITALIAN AGENTS AND SABOTEURS WITH MAJOR BRIAN ROBB.
They are seen aboard an MTB on the way to Chioggia.

'ORSINI.'
One of the two Italian fishing boats on passage to Lussin Piccolo.

On board the Italian fishing boat *Orsini* in the Adriatic on the way from
Termoli to Lussin Piccolo.
Lieut. Bentley-Buckle ensconced in the centre on the cargo of high octane petrol.

# CHAPTER 6
# INTO THE LION'S CAGE

With Termoli as its first base of operations, the exercise to rescue British ex-prisoners began early in November 1943. An advance party under the command of Lt. Bentley-Buckle was to establish a forward position on Lussin Piccolo, one of the many tiny islands off the Dalmatian coast of Jugoslavia just south of Pola. Once secured by Bentley-Buckle's small force, an MTB would use Lussin Piccolo as a staging post for making a series of fast runs across the Adriatic to and from Italian beaches in the regions around Ancona. In the meantime, British agents and Italian partisans were to contact the bands of released prisoners and muster them at rendezvous points on the coast, ready to board the MTB. It was an ambitious and daring plan.

Apart from several partisans, Bentley-Buckle's little force consisted of just ten men and two 60-ft Italian fishing boats, the *Orsini* and the *Lucrezia*. 'B-B', as he was familiarly known, was to ship in the latter along with Worsley, 'Frank' (an American Air Force captain), naval commandos Petty Officer Roberts and Leading Seaman Harrison, and a Jugoslav interpreter named Stepan. In charge of the *Orsini*, much to Worsley's surprise and delight, was none other than his old friend Lt. Guy Morgan, sent up from Malta especially to join the operation. Morgan had with him 'Mac' (a South African Army lieutenant himself recently escaped from an Italian prison camp), and two other naval commandos, Able Seaman Lennan and Able Seaman King. Needless to say, all were volunteers.

The fishing boats, laden literally to the gunwales with stores and equipment and with thousands of gallons of petrol for the expected MTB carried in *yellow* jerry-cans *on deck*, set out from the picturesque little harbour of Termoli at dawn on their hazardous slow passage across waters patrolled by enemy aircraft. Even as they stood out to sea, there was a thunderous barrage of ack-ack fire as a German reconnaisance plane flew low overhead, and Guy Morgan wrote later of that dismal grey morning[*] — 'What the hell was I doing, sitting on 2,500 gallons of high

[*]*Only Ghosts Can Live*, Crosby Lockwood & Son Ltd., London 1945.

octane petrol in the middle of the Adriatic playing at pirates? What would my wife say? I ought to know better at my age . . . ?'

By what at this distance in time might now be regarded as a minor miracle, the fishing boats made their slow crossing of the Adriatic with no further serious incident, and sighted the distinctive hump-backed island of Lussin Piccolo on the morning of the second day. B-B arrived first in *Lucrezia,* having lost *Orsini* at some time during the previous night, and spent several anxious hours on the lookout until the second boat eventually hove into view.

If B-B's party expected a rapturous welcome after their perilous crossing to Lussin Piccolo, they were very quickly disillusioned. They were met on the jetty by what appeared to be a band of scowling brigands, all of them armed to the teeth, and regarded with deepest suspicion. This in spite of the fact that 'Frank' the American was a Special Operations envoy whose mission was to contact and set up liaison lines with the Jugoslav leader, Marshal Tito. Paradoxically, and although they felt themselves virtual prisoners at all times under strict guard, they were housed in a luxurious holiday villa, the property of Captain Guido Cosulich, an Italian millionaire. They were unaware, this first day, that the millionaire's wife and daughter had been peremptorily evicted in order to accommodate them. Afterwards, however, B-B and Co. were grudgingly permitted to entertain — and be entertained by — the signora (Carmen) and her daughter (Noretta) in the comfort of the refugees' own home. The signora, an Anglophile who had in the past been a frequent guest at London's Savoy Hotel, spoke perfect English, and her daughter was an accomplished guitarist, and so they all spent a few pleasant evenings. Food was scarce on the island and the Navy, with several tons of army rations to hand, felt that the least it could do was to see that the ladies were decently fed.

But the week they spent on Lussin Piccolo was by no means all wine and roses. The Jugoslav partisans were controlled by a sort of Committee of Four. They never introduced themselves — their names might probably have been unpronounceable, anyway — and were promptly dubbed 'The Fox', 'Doc', 'Trigger', and 'Flash Harry'. The latter was a gangling youth with straggly long fair hair and a face which not even a mother, much less a naval officer, would trust. He rode a woman's bicycle, was invariably clad in an ankle-length wasp-waisted grey-check overcoat and, like his comrades, always appeared festooned with arms. Pistols, tommy-gun, and bandoliers. He was always 'on the cadge' for something or other: English cigarettes, another pistol and ammunition for same, army rations, and blankets and such. Finally, he announced his intention to come and stay at the villa, and when B-B managed to forestall the suggestion, 'Flash Harry' made it keenly felt that he nursed a fierce and bitter grudge.

'Doc', an equally-sinister figure, peered at the world through thick pebble-glasses. Plump and stolid, pale and stodgy, he would sit throughout 'meetings' in the villa's sumptuous drawing room always in baleful silence, hunched in a shabby raincoat, each of his grimy fat hands carressing the butt of a holstered revolver.

'Foxy', a somewhat older man who might possibly have been In Charge, had precisely that sort of vulpine face which prompted his given nickname. He seldom said very much. He just sat in the corner of a sofa nursing his sub-machine gun and listening carefully, it seemed, to the hesitant phrasings of Stepan, the interpreter.

'Trigger', a young man who affected a para-military battledress complete with forage-cap, appeared as rather less of a threat.

These were the main protagonists at 'meetings' (although others showed up from time to time, and especially at mealtimes) which were not so much meetings as interrogations. The partisans did not trust the Navy, and the feeling was mutual. There was a constant air of ambivalence. It was almost as though the two sides were engaged in direct confrontation as captives and capturers. So much so, indeed, that during one of these encounters B-B leaned over to Worsley and whispered in his ear: 'We should tell them that officers of His Majesty's Royal Navy must never be required to dig their own graves!'

The advance party spent the whole of one week in this uneasy atmosphere, a week of growing worry. Each new day brought an expectation that the promised MTB must arrive, but the MTB was never to appear. Somewhere, somehow, something had gone wrong and the operation had been abandoned, leaving B-B's little group to its fate.

A small but interesting facet of this Lussin Piccolo story is that Lt. Bentley-Buckle had been entrusted at its outset with one hundred British sovereigns, these valuable gold coins to be used to pay for food and shelter in the event of any necessary escape. When the attitude of the Jugoslav partisans made it obvious that such an eventuality might quickly arise, B-B revealed his hoard to his men and gave each of them four coins. The rest, he buried in the garden of the villa, where presumably they remain to this day. Worsley sewed his coins into the flies of his battledress trousers, where they stayed undetected all throughout his incarceration in a German PoW camp and throughout all subsequent trials and tribulations until he was repatriated after the end of the war.

The party's stay at the villa in Lussin was abruptly brought to an end when a German force invaded the island. Worsley and the others were rudely aroused one morning at dawn with the news that enemy landing craft were approaching. In the frantic activity which ensued, Worsley suddenly found himself crouched behind a low wall and shooting as fast as he could work the bolt of a rifle at the foremost German landing barge. He recalls, with a hindsight sense of shame, that not one man on the barge survived to jump ashore on Lussin. But it was very much a case of 'Us or Them', and the Navy soon realised that there were far too many more such landing craft rapidly closing in than they could ever hope to hold off. It was stay and be killed or captured, or try to make a retreat.

B-B chose discretion as the better part of valour, and led his party in a frantic scramble across the mile-wide island. It seemed when they reached the other side that they might be in with a chance. They managed to start the engine of an old diesel motor launch, and all piled in for a crossing to the mainland. It was a brave but useless attempt. The launch was heavily overloaded with Jugoslav partisans crowded on a deck that was almost awash. Nevertheless, they set out on the crossing and it seemed for a little while that perhaps they might just possibly make it. But it was hopeless from the start. German ships which had surrounded the island were backed up by air support, and the launch was attacked by two Arado float planes. Their bombs missed the little boat, but their straffing was much more accurate. Many of the partisans died, most of their bodies hurled overboard by the impact of machine-gun bullets. Their corpses littered the sea all around, and although B-B and his party fought back

*luft beob-
Achtung
7. 11. 4.*

*A.A. Lookout. Skipper in door of wheelhouse
7 Nov. 43*

'LUCREZIA.'

valiantly, rifle fire is of little use against aeroplanes and after twenty desperate minutes of fighting B-B accepted the fact that further resistance amounted to suicide. The Arados were firing armour-piercing bullets which tore through the little craft as though its bulkheads were so much paper, and they were also using incendiary tracers. The launch had been set on fire, and Guy Morgan was wounded with a shattered left forearm. B-B was faced with the age-old question: it was a matter of surrender, or die. B-B saved the lives of his men by opting for the former. He ordered every man left on board to ditch their weapons and hold up their hands.

Now, almost fifty years on, it remains a matter for pause and reflection that the Germans accepted his surrender and so broke off their attack.

B-B's party was taken off the stricken launch and transferred to a German light cruiser, or flak-ship, and treated as prisoners of war. What happened to the surviving partisans might now never be known, because Worsley never saw them again. However, and whatever their fate, the British contingent was treated fairly as legitimate prisoners of war. During their spell of imprisonment on the flak ship they were given the same food as the crew, and Worsley recalls it as being quite good. Guy Morgan's wound was treated by the ship's doctor, and as Morgan states in his book, he never encountered a German doctor who neglected to do his best work regardless of the nationality of his patient.

B-B's party was captured on 13 November, but the flak ship had a further forty-eight hours of patrol still to carry out and it was not until two days later that they were put ashore at Pola, a Jugoslav port on the southern tip of the Bay of Venice. By this time, and in spite of attention from the German naval doctor, Guy Morgan's wounded arm was much worse, swollen from fingertips to elbow. It was a miserable period of discomfort and boredom, and to keep each others' spirits up they reminisced about Termoli, the omnipresent movement of tanks and transports and the constant booming of artillery fire from the front line only a few miles to the north. They recalled the various strange characters they'd met, officers and ratings with secret assignments plotting together by smoky lamplight little wars of their own, landing by night behind the enemy lines, SOE (Special Operations Executive) men, saboteurs and partisans, refugees and just-escaped prisoners. An MTB sneaking up to a dark shore, and hoarsely-whispered calls of 'Good Luck!' as men in a rubber dinghy set out for the beach, and those left on board waiting breathlessly for a sudden brilliant bursting of flares and the rattle of machine-gun fire. Worsley's favourite phrase to describe the heady excitement of these adventures was that they were 'Worth a guinea a box'.

But if this was the worth of their Termoli escapades, they were now to pay the price. After disembarking at Pola the wounded, including Guy Morgan, were separated from the rest of the prisoners and Worsley, Bentley-Buckle, Frank the American, Petty Officer Roberts, and the two Leading Seamen had their first real experience of what it was like to be a prisoner of war. They were put into a large bare cell whose only source of comfort was a scattering of straw on its concrete floor. No bunks, no beds, no chairs or tables and worst of all, no stove. It was mid-November. Winter was setting in, and the six had no greatcoats or any other warm clothing. The nights, especially, were cold, and sleep on the concrete floor was far from long, or restful. Curiously, though, the incident which finally brought home to Worsley the harsh reality of his predicament was the sound of a platoon of German soldiers singing their marching song as they tramped past the cell in the early morning. It was this which shocked him into a realisation that his life was no longer his own.

Mercifully, the incarceration at Pola was temporary, and the six British prisoners were hustled next day into a lorry with a canvas hood for transport to Lubliana. The long and tortuous route wound north over mountains now turning white under a cover of the first winter snows. The lorry was open at the rear and all ten of its passengers, including four armed guards, shivered in the back as the road climbed ever upwards over a series of sharp S-bends. It had soon become evident that none of the Germans could understand a word of English, so the captives were left quite free to discuss their predicament and plot an escape. As the lorry ground steadily higher and higher, B-B pointed out that some of the more-acute bends necessitated a drop in speed to little more than five miles per hour, and went on to suggest that one of their number might possibly jump off and immediately lose himself in the brush and scrub which covered the steep mountainside. They discussed the plan, and it was finally agreed that B-B himself was to make the attempt.

Slowly and casually and with no apparent purpose they gradually shifted position until all six were sitting shoulder to shoulder across the back of the lorry with their legs dangling over the tailboard, ostensibly to admire the magnificent mountain scenery. The German guards sat with their backs against the warmth from the cab, rifles upright between their knees, content to let the mad Englishmen freeze for the sake of enjoying a view. Came the next sharp hairpin bend in the road, B-B whispered 'Now!' and catapulted off the tailboard. Then, scrambling to keep his balance, he hurled himself into the trees and bushes which dropped steeply away from the road. As soon as B-B made his leap the other five closed ranks to form a human blockade, shouting and jumping up and down as though in fright and alarm that one of their number had 'fallen off'. By the time the guards had collected their wits and jumped to the back of the lorry to grab and haul the prisoners apart the escaper was fairly well into cover and tumbling down the mountainside under the force of his headlong momentum. The soldiers began shooting wildly as the lorry jerked to a halt, but none of their shots found its target and B-B got away.

It was a very brave and daring attempt, but one with almost no chance of lasting success. With no known partisan groups in the region, B-B was virtually alone in German-occupied territory, unable to speak the language, and with only vague hope of support. Some of the local inhabitants sympathised with him, and a few offered willing temporary assistance, but most were too afraid to risk their own lives for his safety.

Bentley-Buckle's desperate leap for freedom was made near the village of Moscena. On coming to rest after his rough and tumble plummeting down the mountainside, he buried himself in fallen leaves and lay shivering to wait for darkness. That night he waded an icy river and made his way up into the village, his object being to reach its church unseen. He succeeded, and asked the incumbent for help, but the priest closed the door in his face. In B-B's own words, he 'just didn't want to know'. Turned away from the traditional sanctuary, B-B left Moscena and set off through the night in a persistent deluge of sleet and rain which soaked him down to the skin. About (he thinks) a couple of miles on, he came upon a cottage on the outskirts of a hamlet. Half-frozen and almost exhausted, he tossed small pebbles against the upstairs windows until eventually a light appeared and the owners, an elderly couple, could not have been more kind. They took him in and stripped him and dried him, dressed the cuts and bruises from his tumble down the mountainside, and gave him something warm to eat. Then, they laid a mattress for him along the foot of their bed. Next morning, the wife cut his hair, and it was arranged that he would purchase a bicycle and a set of civilian clothes. A boy from the hamlet guided him over the mountain, and put him on the road to Trieste. When the bicycle punctured he threw it into a ditch and continued his weary way on foot, sleeping that night in a farmyard hayloft. He actually reached Trieste, but was betrayed there and 'sold' to the German Gestapo. He came close to being shot as a spy but instead was delivered — ironically — into the hands of Oberleutnant Helmut Pirner of the S.S. Alpine Division, the army unit responsible for the taking of Lussin Piccolo. Five days after his jump from the lorry, B-B was delivered by Oberleutnant Pirner to the prison in Lubliana, there to re-join Worsley and the others.

Following B-B's leap for freedom, and after the Germans had sorted themselves out, the lorry moved further north into the mountains and made an overnight stop at a pretty little town which Worsley seems to remember as Abatzio. Although the guards were now in a state of high alert, he and Frank were billeted in a small but pleasant hotel and given a nice twin-bedded room. Shortly after being settled in, they received a visit from an English-speaking officer of the Edelweiss Division who brought along a bottle of the local liquor. The officer made no attempt to interrogate them: they all just drank and chatted and afterwards enjoyed the first decent meal they'd had for several days.

Later, mellowed by drink and good food, Frank and Worsley were left alone. As they lay flat on their backs in bed, talking before going to sleep, Worsley's eye was caught by the unusual design of the centre-light fixture. It was, he idly realised, one of the early models the height of which was adjustable. Having always been interested in all things mechanical, Worsley went on as they talked to study how the thing worked and it slowly dawned on him that, in fact, the thing could not possibly work. Curiosity got the better of him, and when he and Frank made a closer examination of the mechanism they found it had been adapted to conceal a microphone. Prompted by this discovery, they went on to make a thorough search of the room, and very soon found two others. It was Worsley's first experience of what we nowadays call 'bugging', and it was one he was never to forget.

They were of course very careful, after finding the bugs, to talk of nothing which might help the Germans. They spent a comfortable night, and in the morning were given a good breakfast. When their 'friend' and Edelweiss officer asked if they'd slept well, Worsley thanked him and said yes, they had, and went on impetuously to commit what he realised later was the serious and unnecessary mistake of making a joke about finding the microphones. The German officer was furious. His former geniality suddenly fell away to be replaced by cold hard enmity, and there was no more kid-glove treatment, no further pretence of being 'nice'.

Officers and ratings were brought together again and placed under heavy guard to make the rest of the journey to Lubliana by train. It was a bitterly cold and hungry trip. There was no heating — or eating — on the train, and heavy falls of snow had covered the ground to a depth of three

or four inches, and the prisoners were still without any warm clothing. When they got off the train at Lubliana they were marched first of all to a German army post, and it was there that Worsley faced a tortuous dilemma. Discussing it later with his fellow inmates of Marlag 'O', it was generally agreed that there is always one time during any period of captivity when the chance to escape occurs.

Worsley's one big chance happened at the Lubliana army post, when he saw an opportunity to duck around the corner of a building and try to reach the woods behind before the guards had noticed his absence. Almost certainly correctly, he chose discretion as the better part of valour, and allowed the chance to slip by. With no food or warm clothing, dressed in Royal Navy battledress, and unable to speak the language of the country, his hopes of remaining long at liberty were practically nil. There was a possibility, also, that the Germans had engineered the opportunity to test his reaction, and he might well have been recaptured within minutes rather than hours or days. So, he passed on the option and was taken forthwith to Lubliana jail.

The prison resembled a medieval fortress with enormously-thick high walls and massive iron gates both within and without locked by old iron keys kept on big iron rings. If the barracks at Pola were grim, Lubliana jail was very much worse. As the prisoners were marched across the inner compound, Worsley was afforded an insight of the weird schizophrenic anomalies existant in the Teutonic mind. Groups of prisoners, about eight to each group, were engaged in clearing snow, shovelling the slush into handcarts. In charge of each group was a fresh-faced youth in the uniform of the S.S. They were armed with long rubber truncheons which they wielded incessantly to belabour the wretches across heads, legs, and shoulders. Such was the age and condition of the unfortunates, it was obvious to Worsley that none had much longer to live, and it was equally

MARLAG 'O' NAVAL OFFICERS' P.O.W. CAMP, WESTERTIMKE, GERMANY 1944.
Christmas 1944: Lieut. 'Blondie' Mewes RNVR decorating the tree (he it was who escaped through 'Albert'). Lieut. Bill Houston Rogers playing the penny whistle. (Houston Rogers was a well known theatre photographer before the war (and after) and also 'Kapellmeister' of the camp orchestra.) Note the stove pipe constructed of Red Cross parcel KLIM milk tins which snaked right round the room to give maximum heat.
*(Imperial War Museum)*

Near Marlag 'O' P.O.W. camp, Westertimke, Germany 1944.
R.A.F. prisoners passing Marlag 'O' having collected wood.
*(Imperial War Museum)*

Funeral from the Merchant Service P.O.W. camp Milag Nord passing Marlag 'O'.
From left: a horse drawn cart hearse, a small party of Milag Nord P.O.W.s, a troupe of German soldiers with a wreath (showing due respect!), German Commandant in horse drawn cab. *(Imperial War Museum)*

MARLAG 'O' P.O.W. CAMP, WESTERTIMKE, GERMANY 1944.
Corner of the camp showing a 'Tiger Box' and German guards (goons) outside the wire. The single wire in the foreground was forbidden to be crossed under threat of shooting. Sometimes 'goons' would beckon 'kriegies' (prisoners) across this wire for bartering purposes, which was, of course, 'verboten'. A particularly evil Feldwebel, probably somewhat mentally deranged from service on the Russian front, enticed a prisoner over one day and then shot him . . . when the war ended, unfortunately for him, he was still with the same prisoners, and he was quietly liquidated'.
*(Imperial War Museum)*

MARLAG 'O' NAVAL OFFICERS' P.O.W. CAMP, WESTERTIMKE, GERMANY 1944.
Camp orchestra playing outside the huts in the summer. 'Kapellmeister' Lieut. Bill Houston Rogers RNVR conducting. From time to time the Swedish Y.M.C.A. would arrive and present a few musical instruments for the camp. Some engineering officers actually made both a very serviceable cello and a double base. They also supplied some artists' materials, and John Worsley used the oil paints to paint Albert's Head.
*(Imperial War Museum)*

STILL LIFE PAINTING OF CANADIAN RED CROSS PARCEL.
The Canadian ones were the most enjoyed, and in the picture is shown a KLIM powdered milk tin which was so valuable, apart from the contents, for making tubes and drinking mugs.
*(Imperial War Museum)*

NAVAL AND ROYAL MARINE P.O.WS ON A FORCED MARCH FROM MARLAG 'O' TO LUBECK AHEAD OF THE ALLIED ADVANCE IN APRIL 1945.
Some of them bartered their Red Cross cigarettes and chocolate with farmers' wives along the way for old ramshackle prams in which to carry their possessions. The column, inspite of having a large Red Ensign draped over the horse cart, was machine gunned by an R.A.F. Typhoon fighter, and six officers were killed. On the extreme left the artist has depicted himself carrying his drawings and paintings in three tin tubes made from the much loved Red Cross KLIM milk tins. *(Imperial War Museum)*

obvious that the youths did not care. He imagined them going home on leave to mothers and wives and sweethearts who in their innocence might never conceive of their mindless brutality. Deeply moved by the incident, he asked his interrogator at the Lubliana prison if he and his fellows might expect the same fate. The interrogator appeared genuinely appalled, and insulted. But of course not, he replied, Worsley and his comrades were *military* prisoners, those out there were *political*. That all in both categories were human beings seemed entirely irrelevant. Yet another unforgettable lesson learned by Worsley.

In the meantime, Bentley-Buckle had been re-captured and returned, as it were, to the fold, and the Britishers were moved from Lubliana prison and put on board a second train for another long, cold, and hungry journey up into Germany and imprisonment there in a Marlag 'O', the one and only German prison camp for naval officers.

The train which carried the prisoners on the first part of their 400-mile journey from Lubliana north through Austria and on to the German capital was crowded with troops, and those which were detailed to guard the prisoners were of a different ilk to the easy-going soldiers who had done so on their previous trips. The one sitting next to Worsley was particularly unpleasant and aggressive and Worsley wished to retaliate in any way he could, although realising his subsequent action was somewhat childish. He realised afterwards that this action was largely ineffective, but capture by an enemy exercises weird effects. It engenders a feeling of helpless frustration, and *anything* one can do to retaliate seems better than doing nothing at all.

It was night, and everyone in the carriage was dozing. On waking up in the early hours of the morning, Worsley saw that the guard sitting beside him appeared to be fast asleep. Very slowly and carefully, he eased the man's bayonet out of its scabbard and then, with the weapon in his hand, was faced with the problem of what to do with it. One bayonet against a train-load of armed troops was worse than nothing at all, so he opened a window and threw the weapon out and settled down to sleep. Next morning, when the party changed trains at a small railway station somewhere in Germany, the prisoners had the satisfaction of seeing the bayonet-less guard receive a furious dressing-down for having 'lost' that piece of his equipment.

The next stage of their journey took them on to Berlin, and they arrived in the early hours of 21 November during the height of what was probably the first-ever 1,000-bomber air raid. It was a staggering experience. The tumultuous devastation was well nigh incredible. Constant thunderous explosions seemed to merge into one horrendous blast which seemed to go on forever. There appeared to be no escape from the onslaught, and the resulting panic was awesome. Military personnel and civilians alike rushed in all directions trying to find shelter, and the prisoners were hustled down a flight of steps into a sort of underground waiting room, where they packed themselves into its furthermost corner.

It was here that the courage of Lt. Anthony Bentley-Buckle manifested itself yet again. As they huddled together, waiting for an end to the blitz, a blazing incendiary bomb fell clattering down the steps. It was a petrifying moment. As the others stared in frozen horror, B-B threw himself forward, grabbed the 'cool' end of the fiercely-burning bomb, and hurled it back up the steps into the deserted concourse. Whether or not

WE LABELLED THEM "THE FOX," "DOC," "TRIGGER" AND "FLASH HARRY."

'THE FOX', 'DOC', 'TRIGGER' AND 'FLASH HARRY.'
Another illustration which appeared in Guy Morgan's book.

the Germans were impressed by such bravery, his prompt action saved them all — captives and captors alike — from a particularly nasty death.

When at long last the Allied bombing subsided, the prisoners were marched across the city to another railway station from whence they were to embark on the final leg of their journey. It was early morning, and in the aftermath of the massive air raid the streets were flanked by burning buildings and fogged by dense clouds of smoke. A rain of fine ashes fell from the sky. There was chaos everywhere. The roads were thronged by distraught civilians, and when it was realised that the men under escort were British the throng became an hysterical mob, and the role of the guards was suddenly reversed. From guarding the prisoners, the escorting soldiers were forced to protect them. One screaming woman broke

through the cordon and spat full into Worsley's face, and as the attacks and abuse continued all were vastly relieved when they finally reached the station and were hustled onto the train which was to take them westwards across the northern part of Germany towards Bremen.

After yet another change of trains at Bremen, the party reached the end of the line at a small town called Tarmstadt and were marched from there to Westetimke, site of two prison camps, the combined Marlags 'M' and 'O', and Milag Nord. In a curious way, they were looking forward to joining a community of their fellows, but this was not to be. Each was placed in solitary confinement in an eight-cell block a little way apart from the main camps, a block which the Germans called *der bunker*.

The two whole months they spent in the bunker, isolated from all contact with each other, was a subtle form of torture. The Germans believed that their seven prisoners — in spite of their having been captured in full uniform — had been operating in Jugoslavia as secret agents, and so were in possession of special knowledge. The solitary confinement was designed to wear them down to a point at which they would be ready to divulge their secrets. It was a process meant to be debilitate the prisoners, to disorientate them and so make them malleable for interrogation. The bare cells were tiny, just 8' x 4', and furnished with nothing but a narrow wooden bunk covered by a thin palliase, and a miniature stove in one corner. Plus, of course, the ubiquitous bucket. They suffered severely from hunger, and cold. They were given one small briquette of brown coal per day, and one bowl of so-called soup.

They were grilled by different Gestapo interrogators twice or three times a week, not one of whom would believe John Worsley when he told them the simple truth; that he was in fact an official War Artist who knew absolutely nothing at all about any of the matters they thought he did. One interrogator appeared to be convinced that Worsley possessed details of 'Hedgehog', one of the Navy's latest weapons. Code-name 'Hedgehog' was a device for the simultaneous launching of a barrage of anti-submarine depth charges. Worsley had heard of the weapon but knew virtually nothing about it. Worn down by incessant questioning, and pressed — if indeed he *was* an artist — to make a drawing of the device, he infuriated his tortmentors by making a sketch of a small prickly animal.

This particular line of questioning was abandoned, but the grillings went on and on and became, in the end, a sort of diversion in endless day after day of stultifying boredom. The prisoners were deprived of everything. Perpetually cold and hungry, they had no human contact other than with their guards; no music, no books to read, nothing with which to divert themselves except their own innermost thoughts.

*No human contact other than that of their guards.* The fact that prisoners kept in isolation eventually come to accept their keepers is a phenomenon now widely accepted. Worsley's regular warders were common soldiers, neither Gestapo nor S.S., and when they heard on the grapevine that Worsley professed to be an artist, one of them provided him with pencil and paper and asked him to draw a pornographic picture. Aware that it might be some sort of 'test', Worsley determined to capitalise on it. He insisted upon a fee for his services, and was rewarded with a whole baked potato. His patron must have been satisfied with the result, because that baked potato was the first of several. Later, when he was provided with paints and paper and asked to create more sophisticated pornography, he upped his fee to a meal of bacon and eggs.

This occasional bonus of extra food helped him to overcome a despair exacerbated by utter loneliness, and among many other deprivations, the crushing humiliation of having to defecate into a stinking hole in the ground with an armed guard standing over him with rifle and fixed bayonet. Worsley's thoughts as he performed this most private of ablutions were that he must surely have hit rock-bottom in the human status, that this must surely be the ultimate degradation.

The physical and mental punishment endured by B-B's party during those eight weeks was of course a clear violation of the Geneva Convention concerning Treatment of Prisoners, and their German tormentors were well aware of the fact. Ironically, it afforded them an opportunity to inflict upon the seven men a cruel hiatus in their ordeal. One morning, they were taken from the bunker and marched out of the camp to a similar little cell block which was hidden out of sight in the woods. They were left in that freezing cold place all day, and returned to the bunker that same evening. No explanations were given, but they were later to learn the reason for their brief transfer. A delegation from the Swedish Red Cross had been to inspect conditions at Westetimke, and the bunker had been evacuated in order that it might be seen to be empty.

But the devastating effect of being thrown back in the bunker was only the start of much worse. At the end of his next interrogation, Worsley's oppressors hinted to him that he was likely to be taken out next morning and shot, that he had been judged to be a spy and would probably be executed as such. He remembered his reaction as being calm and philosophical. He knew that many hundreds of thousands had died in that grim war, and he counted himself as just one more of that number. He does not doubt that a great many of these derived solace from a belief in God, but he did not seek such comfort. In his own words: 'I can see no evidence in this world of any Deity which appears to have concern for the welfare of Life, whether human, animal, or vegetable, and the frequent arbitrary horrors which occur would seem to support my conviction. There may indeed be a power of some kind responsible for the magnificence of our incredible universe and all that happens in it, but if so, it appears to have no regard for living things.' He had always endeavoured to behave in a decent and proper manner during his uncompleted life, and was prepared to accept his threatened fate if that was what it had to be. All he hoped was that the process would not be too painful.

The fact that death by firing squad was not to be his fate is evidenced by the fact that he remains very much alive to this day. The interrogators' threat was an empty bluff, a sort of last resort. But Worsley could not tell the Germans anything, because he knew nothing to tell. He still does not know, and will now never know, what finally persuaded them that B-B's party had no secret information, but he blesses that visit by the Swedish Red Cross because those good people *knew* that Royal Navy Lieutenants Bentley-Buckle, Guy Morgan, and John Worsley, and the two leading seamen had been captured, and their continued disappearance would have proved embarrassing. So all were spared their fate and transferred, at the end of two months of cold and hunger and suffering in the bunker, to the 'comfort' of Marlags 'O' and 'M'.

**MTB**
This drawing was made just before John Worsley's capture and shows various agents and saboteurs on board an MTB on their way to be landed on Cioggia beach in November, 1943 . . . the drawing was made on an old discarded Naval chart. *(Courtesy of Peter Chasseaud.)*

LIEUT. DOUGLAS WOODS RNR.
He organised all distributions of, and catering with, Red Cross parcels.

# CHAPTER 7
# MARLAG 'O'

Marlags 'O' and 'M' at Westertimke, some twelve miles from Bremen, comprised the only German P.O.W. camp ever used for the incarceration of Royal and Allied Navies' personnel. Marlag 'O' held about 400 officers, Marlag 'M' about 2,000 ratings of other ranks. The two sections were separated by a wide corridor flanked by barbed wire, which enclosed an administration and barracks block for German officers. The shower house used by all ranks for their weekly bath was perhaps a third of a mile outside the main compound. Marlag Nord, another camp situated about a mile away, housed a much larger contingent of merchant navy prisoners, around 10,000 officers and men, and a number of luckless civilian passengers.

Out from under their threat of execution, Worsley and Bentley-Buckle were released from solitary confinement and allocated bunks in a room in one of the six big Marlag 'O' huts. There were ten or twelve men to a room, eight rooms in each hut. Also, there was one large mess hut, and another of similar size lined inside with rows of unpartitioned lavatory bowls and washbasins. The only other feature of the Marlag 'O' was a sizeable artificial pond for use as a water supply in the event of fire. In fact, the pond was commonly used for the sailing of model yachts made by the prisoners from any scrap of material which might possibly be employed, virtually every single item of which was provided by the International Red Cross.

The I.R.C. did a wonderful job for prisoners of war of all sides. Workers from neutral Sweden and Switzerland traced and ascertained the whereabouts of individual servicemen, informed the relevant authorities, and went on to succour the unfortunates by delivering letters and packages from home and by transporting and sometimes providing the necessities and small luxuries of life. On the calendars of P.O.Ws, Red Cross days were red-letter days, and absolutely nothing was ever wasted. Paper and string from personal parcels, wood from the communal crates, emptied tins and cardboard cartons — all were carefully hoarded against possible future use. Timber from the crates was turned into chairs and armchairs. Any fragments left over were used to build model boats, and a wide variety of other small artefacts. The ingenuity of men whose natural creative urge is inhibited by captivity is truly astonishing. The inmates of Marlag 'O' pooled their collective skills to make, among many other things, an assortment of musical instruments which included a cello and a double-bass. They even built a record-player.

Every single fragment of material was put to some kind of use, but empty tins were prized above rubies. Their uses were infinite, whether carefully opened top and bottom and left cylindrical, or cut sideways and hammered flat. In the cylindrical mode, empty Canadian KLIM dried

TYPICAL 'ROOM.'
Note the double bunk at top left with a home-made shelf at its end . . . Red Cross parcel packing case armchairs and home-made gramophone in the foreground.

milk tins, always the favourite, were used by Worsley to design and build a central-heating system. Every room had a little stove, but the ration of fuel was grossly inadequate. When prisoners went to bed, they didn't *un*dress, quite the opposite; they donned every item of clothing they possessed. It was that or wake up extremely cold, because once the daily ration of fuel was spent there wasn't any more to be had until the next day's issue. They had to extract every unit of heat from every last ounce of coal.

Originally, the stove-pipes went straight up through the roofs of the huts, and vented hot air into the great outdoors. KLIM milk tins changed all that. Worsley joined scores if not hundreds end-in-end to form a 'pipe' which ran all around the room, and by the time the hot air which emanated from the stove escaped into the atmosphere it was no longer hot, because almost every particle of heat had been dissipated within the room. It has been said that 'Necessity is the Mother of Invention', and never was this more true than in P.O.W. camps everywhere.

It would be impossible to exaggerate the enormous comfort bestowed upon prisoners, of all factions, by the International Red Cross and the Swedish Y.M.C.A.* Aside from providing crates of durables such as books, sheet music, musical instruments, gramophone records, etc., they provided every single man with individual food parcels. The contents varied according to the nationality of the donors, but although each and every one was treasured, those from Canada were generally voted best of all. Worsley made a still-life painting of the contents of one typical Canadian parcel. (q.v.): tins of KLIM dried milk, corned beef, chopped pork, and butter, packets of raisins and of prunes, a large block of chocolate, and soap and cigarettes. Occasional luxuries such as these made camp-life tolerable, and formed a vital supplement to the vitamin deficient prison food. They were also invaluable currency for barter, and for bribing the German guards.

Worsley recalls one such illegal transaction which ended catastrophically. He and his room-mates had pooled their resources to make a major trade involving several bottles of good-quality schnapps. The opportunity to do so occurred in the summer of 1944, but the liquor was not for broaching, it was to be hidden and saved for a celebration party at Christmas. The bottles were buried outside under one of the room's windows, safe from prying eyes, but one vital factor had been overlooked: the ground was frozen solid and in the attempt to dig them up, one of the precious bottles was broken.

Boredom and despair were the omnipresent twin evils of any P.O.W. camp, and the inmates of Marlag 'O' contrived in many ways to keep themselves occupied and amused. The chief organiser of camp entertainments was Lieutenant Bill Houston Rogers, R.N.V.R. Houston Rogers had been a theatre photographer before the war, and was to become widely celebrated in that profession on his return to civilian life. In the meantime, he organised regular diversions in the forms of orchestral and variety concerts, amateur dramatics, etc. An excellent amateur musician himself, he formed a camp orchestra, and held teaching classes. He cajoled and schooled and encouraged performers, and his contribution to the maintenance of morale was one of significant importance.

*This did not include Japan. Prisoners of the Japanese were subjected to obscenities almost beyond belief, and only a tiny minority survived.

It is now a fact of history that 1944 marked a turning point in World War Two. One-thousand-bomber raids on Germany had become a regular occurrence, evidence of which was plainly visible to the inmates of Marlag 'O'. They congregated outside in the compound during the many daylight raids, every man with his head thrown back anxiously to watch the battle being waged in the sky, the vapour-trails created by Flying Fortresses and the myriad of cotton-wool puffs which marked the explosions of anti-aircraft shells. There were numerous such occasions, because it seemed that the Royal and U.S. Air Forces used the prison camp as a ground-marker for their run-in on the strategic target of Bremen, only twelve miles further on.

Worsley still nurtures enormous respect for the bravery of those American airmen who manned the B-17s. There were many casualties. Each Flying Fortress had a crew of ten, and when one of the 'planes suffered a hit, the Marlag 'O' observers held their collective breath as, hopefully, the canopies of parachutes began to blossom in the sky. The count was shouted out in unison, and each time *ten* was reached, the number was followed by a resounding cheer. The satisfaction was two-fold: it was manifest of huge relief, and it vastly irritated the German guards. Sadly, of course, there were occasions when no parachutes appeared in the sky.

But in the meantime, life in the camp went on. Worsley and Bentley-Buckle had become accepted as bona fide members of The Room, although the interrogations they had suffered in the bunker did not necessarily cease upon their release from that grim place. They were immediately subjected to others, albeit of a different kind. First, an 'interview' with the senior officer, (Captain Micklethwaite, R.N.) who questioned them in a civil manner as to who and what they were, and how they were captured, and where, and when. These were the routine 'official' questions. Those posed later by room-mates were much more casual, but equally incisive. Off-hand references to old ships and old shipmates, family and lifestyle at home, and enquiries regarding possibly mutual acquaintances. All designed, of course, to establish unimpeachable credentials. Like every other P.O.W. community, the prisoners of Marlag 'O' were automatically suspicious of new arrivals. Always fearing a German 'plant', they trusted no-one until they were convinced beyond all doubt that the newcomer was precisely who he purported to be.

Once accepted into a Room, the newcomer became part of a small but exceptionally close-knit community. Although an integral section of the hut, and by extension of the camp at large, every Room was a separate entity with a 'character' all of its own. Its occupants lived literally on top of each other on rows of two-tier bunks, so that 'when one turned over, all turned over'. Similar overcrowding of living space sometimes breeds paranoia and madness in rats, and it is a tribute to Man's spirit of endurance that the human animal was able to adapt so successfully.

Much of Worsley's personal comfort derived from occasional Red Cross gifts of brushes and colours, both oil and water, and paper and paper-board, which he kept in cannisters fashioned from KLIM cans. These he also used for storing his finished drawings and paintings. Canvas, however, seemed unobtainable, and although he possessed a supply of oil paints he lacked any medium for their useful employment. But the problem was not insoluble. At some time previously, the Room

LIEUTENANT GODFREY PLACE VC, RN. (NOW REAR ADMIRAL PLACE, VC, CB, DSC)
He received his VC for mining the German battleship *Tirpitz* in Alten Fjord, Norway in 1943 from a midget submarine. Painted on a piece of German linen sheet in Marlag 'O' Naval P.O.W. camp, Germany 1944. (Now hanging in the National Maritime Museum, Greenwich.)

LIEUTENANT DONALD CAMERON VC, RNR.
He also received the award for mining the German battleship *Tirpitz* in Alten Fjord,
Norway in 1943 from a midget submarine. Painted on a piece of German linen sheet in
Marlag 'O' Naval P.O.W. camp, Germany 1944. (Now hanging in the National Maritime
Museum, Greenwich.)

had resolved to barter with the guards for a pair of very fine linen sheets, the object being to make colourful curtains with which to brighten up the Room. Worsley had carved linocuts from scraps of linoleum to create a floral design, and using his limited colours had produced a cheering effect. A consensus of opinion in the Room was that the curtains be sacrificed.

The decision was justified by a proposal that Worsley should paint three important portraits of men who had been awarded the Victoria Cross. The three V.C.s whose portraits were painted during their imprisonment in Marlag 'O' included Lt. (later Rear Admiral) B. G. C. Place R.N., and Lt. Donald Cameron R.N.R., two of the heroes of Altenfiord.

Arctic convoys carrying armaments and supplies vital to Russia's war effort had to be discontinued in February 1943, because German naval and air forces stationed on the southern flank of their long route around North Cape made the risk of sinking unacceptable. By far the most serious threat to the convoys was represented by a powerful German naval squadron which included the great Battleships *Tirpitz* and *Scharnhorst*, and at least ten destroyers, stationed in the apparently-impregnable shelter of Norway's Altenfiord. The narrow fiord was so heavily protected by mines and anti-submarine nets that an attack from the sea was considered virtually impossible, and the anchorage was beyond the reach of R.A.F. heavy bombers. An attack by the Fleet Air Arm was equally impractical, as the Home Fleet's only aircraft carrier, the old HMS *Furious*, lacked the strike-capability to have any hope of success.

As the situation in Russia became ever more desperate, strategists at the Admiralty racked their brains for a solution to the dilemma, and finally came up with a plan of staggering audacity. Operation code-name 'Source' called for penetration of the German defences by midget submarines, known as X-craft. These little 35-ton vessels carried a four-man crew and were loaded with explosives to be placed on the sea-bed beneath the target, and detonated by a time fuse. It was thought that the tiny submersibles stood a fair chance of forcing their way under or through the German defences, planting their charges beneath *Tirpitz* and *Scharnhorst*, and getting safely out again before the explosives went off.

On 11–12 September 1943 six regular submarines sailed from their base in north-east Scotland, each with a 'baby' in tow, but one of the X-craft was lost with all hands on the long northern passage, and another suffered so badly she had to be abandoned. The other four cast off from their mother ships on the 20th, and set out to penetrate what was probably the most impregnable harbour of all time. The parent vessels lay submerged at the offshore rendezvous in the hope of picking up the crews, if not the craft, when their mission had been carried out. It was a somewhat desperate hope. The anchorage lay deep into the fiord, protected by 50 miles of defences in the form of minefields and undersea steel nets. At some time during the following night, X-5 lost contact with the others, and was never heard of again. The remaining three pressed ahead, and by the early hours of the 22nd, X-6 and X-7, commanded respectively by Lieutenants Cameron and Place, were in position for their final approach to the *Tirpitz*. In the meantime, X-10 had suffered severe damage on her way up the fiord and her captain, without compass or periscope, had been compelled to abandon his assault on the *Scharnhorst* and make his way out to sea. He was successful in reaching a rendezvous with his waiting submarine, but X-10 was lost with all hands in heavy weather during the course of her long tow home.

Poised as they were on the final stage of their attack, both Cameron and Place encountered last-minute setbacks. X-6 developed serious faults in its periscope, and X-7 became entangled in the defensive nets. Both overcame their difficulties, but in doing so X-6 was forced to break surface and was spotted by the enemy. The captain of *Tirpitz* immediately shifted his cables in order to move his ship as far away as possible, but Cameron groped his way after her and placed two high-explosive charges directly beneath his huge target. Having done so, he surfaced again, promptly scuttled X-6, and he and his crew were picked up and taken on board the battleship. As this was happening, Lt. Place had managed to submerge again and to set his charges along with Cameron's directly under *Tirpitz*'s vast hull. Mission accomplished, he tried to force his way back through the nets, but was still impossibly entangled when at 08:12 that morning the huge explosions occurred, and his midget sub was so badly affected he was forced to abandon ship. Only he and one other of the four-man crew escaped the devastating blast, but the *Tirpitz* was blown almost out of the water with damage so severe she was never again a threat to Arctic convoys.

So it was that Lieutenants Cameron and Place ended up in Marlag 'O', and had their portraits painted on the backs of linen curtains. Both hang now in the National Maritime Museum at Greenwich and, given permission, the viewer might turn them around and see on the backs a second work by Worsley: — the lino-printed floral design.

The other sitter of Worsley's three V.C. portraits won his prestigious award in an action which pre-dated that of Altenfiord. This time, his subject was fellow Marlag 'O' inmate, Lt. Commander S. H. Beattie, R.N., another incredibly brave man. Beattie distinguished himself in the famous Raid on St. Nazaire, as captain of the destroyer HMS *Campbeltown.*

Although it took place eighteen months earlier, the action at St. Nazaire had much to do with the threat from *Tirpitz*. The mighty German battleship could not lurk indefinitely in her lair at Altenfiord, just waiting to pounce upon Allied convoys to Russia. She had to re-fit and re-provision, and the only way to deny her this facility was to destroy thoroughly the only dock in western France with lock-gates big enough to afford her a safe haven in occupied France. *Ergo*, the docks at St. Nazaire must be destroyed. The solution was perfectly obvious, but the means by which it might be achieved was quite another matter, and the plan which eventually emerged involved the Chief of Combined Operations. It required the closest of co-operation between Army and Navy commandos, both of which services must embark on a near-suicidal venture.

The attack on St. Nazaire was conceived as a desperate gamble by men, far removed from the fray, who had everything to win yet nothing to lose but an ageing ex-American destroyer and a number of small coastal craft. Including, of course, the men on board. This which follows is a brief account of what actually happened at or about 01:30 in the morning of 28 March 1942. There were many such actions during those long years of conflict but this, too, has relevance here insofar as it concerns John Worsley's War.

A strike force consisting of HMS *Campbeltown* and eighteen small

LIEUT. CDR. 'SAM' BEATTIE VC, RN.
Received the award when, as Captain of HMS *Campbeltown*, he rammed and blew up the Normandie dock gate during the St Nazaire raid of 28 March, 1942. Painted on a piece of German linen sheet in Marlag 'O' Naval P.O.W. camp, Germany 1944. (Now hanging in the National Maritime Museum, Greenwich.)

coastal craft set out from Falmouth on 26 March, led by Commander R. E. D. Ryder, R.N. Ryder was in motor gun boat MGB 314, skippered by Lt. D. M. C. Curtis R.N.V.R., together with the officer in charge of Army commandos, Colonel A. C. Newman. The *Campbeltown* was packed with many tons of time-fused high explosive, and the task of Sam Beattie was to ram the massive lock-gates, and then discharge 260 commandos whose job it would be to blow up the lock-gates' operating machinery before retiring, along with *Campbeltown*'s crew, to re-embark in the fleet of small launches for a passage back out to sea.

St. Nazaire lies on the Loire, five miles upstream of the river mouth. Commander Ryder led his little fleet into the estuary after dark on the 27th and succeeded, by a series of skilful deceptions, so to confuse the enemy defences that his vessels encountered no serious retaliation until its objective was reached and HMS *Campbeltown* rammed the huge lock-gates, thrusting her bows clean through and jamming them fast against its concrete sides. This was at or about 1:30 am on the 28th, and the tremendous charges with which she was filled were timed to explode ten hours later, at noon. (They did so, and inflicted very heavy casualties on the Germans who had gone on board to inspect her.) But by this time Cdr. Ryder's task force was under a maelstrom of fire, and although the commandos in *Campbeltown* were able to leap ashore, those on board the launches were prevented from joining them. All but two of the sixteen small craft were destroyed. The raid lasted almost two hours, every minute of which was filled with tremendous opposing fire, and it remains a minor miracle that Cdr. Ryder's MGB managed to come alongside the dock and rescue many of the *Campbeltown*'s crew. Most of the soldiers put ashore had to be left behind, but weighed against the enormous success of the operation — the lock-gates were completely destroyed — the casualty count of 170 killed and missing was considered remarkably light.

Aside from his portrait of Lt. Commander Beattie, V.C., John Worsley later painted two striking canvasses of the Raid on St. Nazaire. The first showing *Campbeltown* rammed fast in the lock-gates, was commissioned by Lord Newborough and now hangs in one of the staterooms of Her Majesty's Royal Yacht *Britannia* and is on the jacket of this book. The second, commissioned by Lady Newborough, with *Campbeltown* in the background, shows the motor torpedo boat MTB 74 commanded by Sub. Lt. R.C.M.V. Wynn, R.N.V.R. (now Lord Newborough) torpedoeing the dock entrance to the U-boat basin.

Another of Worsley's Marlag 'O' portraits features the camp's senior officer, Captain 'D' — i.e. commander of a squadron of destroyers — Micklethwaite, R.N., and lacking any other medium upon which to paint it, the Room agreed that Worsley might use one of the ceiling-boards which served in small part as its meagre insulation. During the period of Worsley's work, the Room was subjected to an icy draught from the missing panel, and once the painting was done, the panel was replaced and there it remained  throughout the life of Marlag 'O', admired by guards and prisoners alike. It is a curious reflection upon the diversity of national attitudes that the German guards who came to look up at the painting regarded their charges as quite mad.

Prisoners of war were sustained throughout their ordeal each in his own special way. Almost all became introspective with private dreams of Home, but the one universally-recognised factor was that all were in the same boat, and that all must stick together. Life in a prison camp

contradicted the concept of 'Every man an island, complete within himself'. It subscribed wholeheartedly to a common existence, and an over-riding determination to *live*. Some individuals occupied their minds by making music, or model boats, or writing on the crinkly grey German lavatory paper, or nurturing little patches of garden with seeds provided by the Red Cross, or devising heating systems, or the best means of bartering with guards, and so on *ad infinitum*. But all of these divertisements were subject to a common cause composed of two vital elements: survival, and escape.

MAKING A MODEL YACHT.

THE WORKSHOP HUT, MARLAG 'O'.

It is a little-known fact that although the present Geneva Convention for the care and protection of prisoners-of-war was not signed by the 58 governments concerned until 12 August 1949, its proposals had long been accepted by all but the Japanese. The original draft of the Geneva Convention, proposed by a committee of the International Red Cross in 1864, was never properly ratified, but the attendant representatives of 28 nations unanimously agreed to observe the basic human rights of prisoners. One of the clauses enshrined in the Convention allowed *every* prisoner-of-war to attempt his escape from the enemy with no fear of retribution should his attempt be foiled. To attempt an escape was every man's *duty*: it was also his internationally-recognised right.

So it was that much of the collective brain-power assembled in

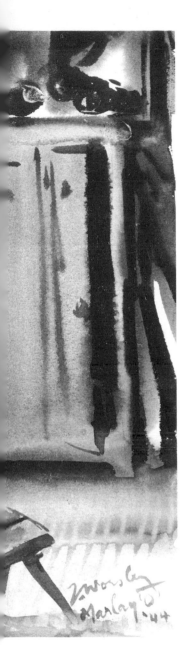

Marlag 'O' was concentrated on means of escape. Tunnelling at different levels went on all the time, but escape by this means proved simply impossible. The entire complex of Marlags 'O' and 'M' had been surrounded by a very deep water-filled ditch, and as the region's water-table was so extremely high that tunnel after tunnel quickly became engulfed. But most were discovered before becoming waterlogged, because the ground above was so soft it soon collapsed on the surface and so gave the game away to the omnipresent patrolling guards. Some few optimists continued to tunnel deeper but their efforts were largely therapeutic, and none came to any avail.

It is interesting to note at this point that of all the prisoners in Marlag 'O', there was only one with no need to break out. Worsley's old friend Lt. Guy Morgan had eventually been sent to the camp, and although he was in a different Room they saw each other every day. In spite of German medical attention, his wounded arm refused to heal, and was still encased in plaster from wrist to elbow. There was talk of his being repatriated in a not-uncommon exchange for a wounded German counterpart, and negotiations through the medium of the Protecting Power* were already well in hand. It seemed it would only be a matter of time before Morgan was on his way home.

As the great day approached, the chums faced a problem. Morgan had written an account of their escapade at Lussin Piccolo, and Worsley had made a number of sketches to illustrate the embryonic book. The question was, how to smuggle both manuscript and sketches out of Marlag 'O' and carry them safety back to England? Morgan was sure to be searched, and his meagre personal possessions afforded no hiding place. The dilemma was finally resolved with typical prison-camp ingenuity. Morgan's shattered arm had withered considerably inside its plaster cast, and the carefully-folded papers were packed inside all around the shrunken limb. The hiding place was never discovered. Guy Morgan eventually published his book, and Worsley's sketches were reproduced in it.

The second most obvious escape route lay, of course, through the wire, but this too appeared virtually impossible. The formidable barrier was constructed in four parts, the first being a single yard-high strand placed five yards back from the innermost of two tall fences. This acted as a sort of warning wire. The constant patrols and the machine-gunners up in the watch towers, or tiger boxes, had orders to shoot any prisoner the instant he stepped over the wire into the five-yard strip of no-go area between it and the first high fence. This sixteen-foot lattice of heavy barbed wire was topped by a supplementary section which sloped inwards at an angle of 45 degrees, and the further five-yard gap which separated it from its identical twin was crammed with a tangle of coils bearing innumerable razor-sharp spikes.

Such was the situation in 1944. There had previously been one escape by this route, when a R.N.V.R. lieutenant broke through and actually made his way back to England, but the wire had since been reinforced, and although Marlag 'O' was not a Castle Colditz it was the Commandant's proud boast that there had never been a subsequent escape. That, however, was before John Worsley arrived on the scene.

*An impartial Authority with powers to inspect conditions in any prison camp of whatever nationality (except Japanese) and to insist upon proper treatment of prisoners according to the Articles of the Geneva Convention.

One of the many contradictions between the stark realities of Marlag 'O' and the stage and film fictions it subsequently inspired concerned a second attempted escape through the wire. The British kriegies — an abbreviation of *kriegsgefangenen,* the German word for prisoners-of-war — were joined towards the end of 1944 by a captured American serviceman, a Major of Marines. It happened that, in peacetime, the major had been a Hollywood stuntman, a fact which he instantly announced to back up his boast that he would be out of Marlag 'O' within a matter of weeks. His intention was to cut a way through the wire during one of the frequent Allied air raids, the only time at night when the powerful tiger box floodlights were switched off, so pitching the camp into darkness.

It was of course essential that any attempt at escape be subject to consideration by the Escape Committee, and approved by its chairman, the senior officer. After due deliberation, the American was granted permission to go ahead with his plan. But that was only the start of the operation: once approved, the *real* work began. To escape successfully from the camp was quite useless in itself. Any movement outside was

INSIDE A TUNNEL.
Note the system of lighting with an electric light in a bottle. The drawing is of necessity rough and scrappy having been done in the confined space.

Inside P.o.w. Tunnel. 44

92

almost as difficult as movement within. The escaper needed money, and documents, and a supply of the basic foods sufficient to sustain him over days, or even weeks. With the war fast approaching a desperate climax — desperate for Germany, that is — all human traffic was severely restricted. It was impossible to board a train or a bus without first producing a travel permit and proofs of identity, and lacking such 'genuine' pieces of paper the would-be escapee might just as well be back in captivity. Every single escape involved an enormous volume of logistics.

The prison camp of Marlag 'O' was more fortunate than most in that it housed a cornucopia of talent. Its team of forgers, which included John Worsley, was probably the best, and once the American's plan was approved the team applied itself to the job of providing him with documents by far the most important of which was the basic Identity Card *with photograph*. Using a fine soft pencil, Worsley spent all of three weeks creating a 'photograph' of the American and laminating the drawing with a layer of cellophane salvaged from a cigarette packet. He further enhanced his miniature masterpiece by reproducing, with pen and

DIGGING INSIDE A TUNNEL.

ink, an official swastika stamp complete with date and place of issue and signed by an 'authority'. Worsley's was by no means the only effort; others of the team were at work faking *typewritten* papers in *pencil*. Incredible, but perfectly true. A separate band of conspirators was detailed to tempt the guards into parting with German money in exchange for cigarettes, and tins of real butter, and bars of chocolate. A truly exemplary case of 'All for one, and one for all.'

After several weeks of communal effort, the American was made ready to depart, the only remaining requirement being another Allied air raid, and a switching-off of the floodlights. He did not have long to wait, and he actually succeeded in breaking through the wire. But with freedom in his grasp, he ran no more than a hundred yards before being caught by the hounds of the omnipresent dog-patrol. He was set upon by the dogs, and with their keepers closing in on him he dutifully followed the drill by immediately chewing and swallowing his forged papers. First his 'identity card', and Worsley's three weeks of meticulous work was consigned in about three seconds flat to the American's digestive tract. His very gallant venture having failed, the Major of Marines was dragged back into the camp, still chewing and gulping the rest of his 'papers'.

Stage and film portrayals of life in Marlag 'O' have had an escaper being shot. In fact, this never happened. What actually *did* happen was very much worse. The 'no go' rule applicable to the area between the yard-high inner wire and the first perimeter fence was commonly permitted to go by the board. The German guards patrolling that stretch would themselves disregard the rule. Those who had something to barter for chocolate or cigarettes would often invite a prisoner to step across the wire, in order that they might do business. It happened from time to time, and no-one thought anything of it. Until, that is, the day came when one particular German guard, a positively evil wretch, indicated by beckoning that he wished to make a trade. The eager kriegie stepped over the wire, and the instant that he did, his seducer cut him down with machine-gun fire. This atrocity was neither forgotten nor forgiven, and when the end of the war brought liberation to the room-mates of the murdered man, they exacted a summary justice. The bestial guard was still there. The room-mates sought him out, and shot him.

But that was to come in the future, and in the meantime of 1944 the Marlag 'O' Escape Committee was racking its collective brains to find an alternative to tunnelling, and the wire. Successive meetings offered no solution until one day Worsley said:

'I know! I'll make a dummy!'

It was an off-the-cuff idea, not much more than a flight of fancy, but once he had blurted it out, Worsley felt himself committed and it became incumbent on him to develop the notion and work out the details. He knew it would take much time, but time is the one commodity of which all prisoners-of-war enjoyed an endless surfeit. So Worsley had plenty of time in which to think how a dummy might work. The concept having been achieved, he was faced by the problem of its birth, and fruition. The practicalities of the scheme seemed insurmountable, to say nothing of its effective employment. But every single human innovation since a wise old Greek shouted *Eureka!* has been founded on spontaneous thought and so it was that Albert, R.N., was conceived and brought about, and *made* to work so successfully.

NAVAL OFFICERS FILLING IN A DISCOVERED TUNNEL.

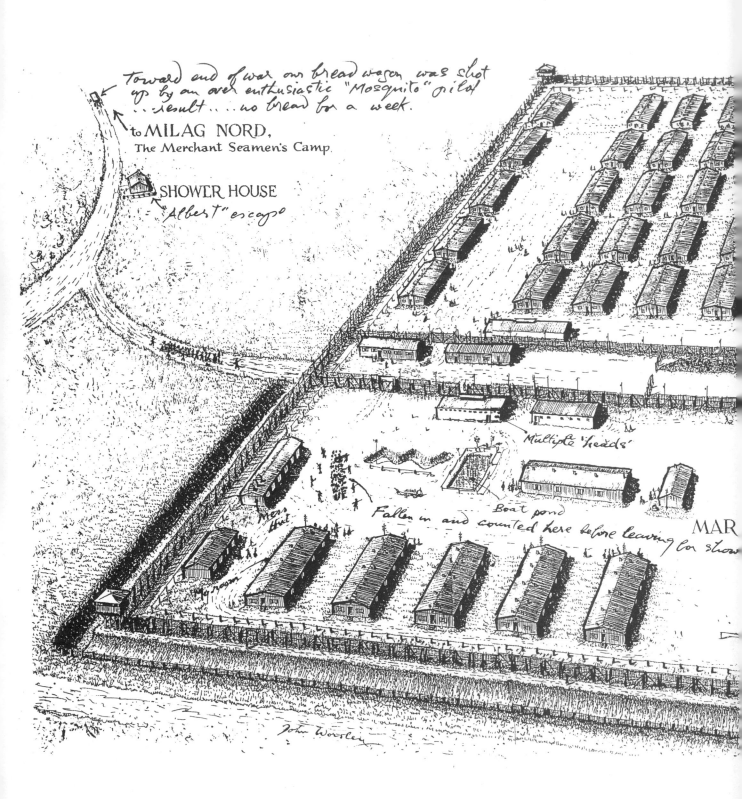

Toward end of war our bread wagon was shot up by an over enthusiastic "Mosquito" pilot ... result ... no bread for a week.

to MILAG NORD,
The Merchant Seamen's Camp.

SHOWER HOUSE
"Albert" escape

Multiple 'heads'

Boat pond

Fallen in and counted here before leaving for show

Mess hut

MAR

John Worsley

96

# CHAPTER 8
# ALBERT, R.N.

'ALBERT R.N.'

The story of Albert, R.N., has been the subject of fictional portrayals in story, on stage, and on screen. This which follows is the definitive account straight, as it were, from the horse's mouth.

Worsley's idea was to use his dummy officer as a substitute for the genuine article following one of the prisoners' weekly visits to the bath house, which was situated roughly half way between Marlag 'O' and Milag Nord. Every Thursday afternoon, the inmates of Worsley's Room were mustered, along with others in the compound, in columns of three. When the guards had made a head-count, they were marched through the gate into the German Admin. block compound, where they were counted a second time before being marched through the outer gate and up the road to the shower house. After completing their ablutions they were formed up and counted again, before being marched back into the camp and submitted to a final count. So many out, same number back in.

It will be seen that in order to have any hope of success, Albert must fulfil two vital functions: he had to be entirely collapsible, and he had to be wonderfully realistic. How to achieve these essential qualities with the very limited resources available presented problems of large dimensions. Aided and abetted by his friend and room-mate Lt. Bob Staines, R.N.V.R., Worsley set to work. Bob Staines began to make Albert's body-cage, while Worsley created Albert's head.

He began with scraps of cloth, which he sewed together to form a bag the size and shape of a skull. This was then stuffed with straw and kapok to serve as a removable base over which to build up layers of papier mache, excellent materials for which were unwittingly provided by their captors. The prisoners were given regular copies of a German propaganda newspaper called the *Volkischer Beobachter* and this, pulped together with size obtained from guards by barter, was perfect for the job. By an enormously painstaking process of building-up and sanding-down layer upon layer of papier mache, Worsley gradually sculpted the features. A famous monthly magazine once ran a series of articles entitled 'The Most Unforgettable Character I've Ever Met!' Worsley's object was to achieve the opposite: his aim was to make the image of a *most forgettable* man.

Albert's hair and eyebrows were obtained by clipping locks from the heads of his real live room-mates. The top of his head was left bald, because he was always to wear his officer's cap. The delicate tints of his face were painted using the tubes of oil colours donated by the Swedish Y.M.C.A. who also provided the ping-pong ball cut in half to form his eyes. Various other of his essential components were made from materials originating in Canadian Red Cross parcels. It might be said of Albert that he was a truly international man.

Worsley's efforts did not end with an astonishingly lifelike head. He spent endless hours on the design and perfection of a most ingenious device by means of which Albert, a cigarette in mouth, was made to move his eyelids. The corners of his eyelids were mounted on tiny pin bearings, and a lateral axle fixed across inside the head carried a small cylinder made from a Red Cross parcel salmon tin with a wooden centre. The cylinder was revolved by a pendulum with ratchet which swung as Albert was carried along. There were two nails sticking out of the perimeter of the tin which, as it slowly revolved, tripped a flange connected to the eyelids and made them occasionally blink. Aside from his consummate skills as an artist, Worsley was an inventive engineer. With the papier mache skull set hard, the straw and kapok stuffing was removed in order to facilitate work on this interior mechanism.

As his head was taking shape, so was the rest of Albert's anatomy. His trunk was a sturdy wire cage stitched into the lining of an officer's greatcoat in such a clever way that the coat could be worn by one of the prisoners as they marched up the road to the baths. Fixtures at either side of the cage supported a lateral wooden bar from which the legs were hung. These and various other components — including of course the head — were concealed by the kriegies on their way to the showers in their bundled-up bath towels which also served to conceal the escaper's civilian clothes, and food. Albert had no hands, because few of the P.O.W.s owned gloves and most walked around with their hands in their pockets. Once assembled, Albert was supported by two sets of hooks which fitted over the arms of his 'minders' — Lieutenants Worsley and Staines — one of them on either side.

When at last Albert was finally completed, intensive training began. Numerous rehearsals in which he was assembled and dismantled were carried on and on until the teamwork involved came as close to perfection as it was ever likely to be, and Albert's impending debut raised the burning question: which member of the Room would be the first one to test his efficacy? There existed an unwritten rule that the originator of any escape plan had an inalienable right to exercise prerogative, but if Worsley 'went away' who then would be capable, should the device succeed, of masterminding successive usage of Albert? But this was only one of other and perhaps more weighty considerations. Really  good escape devices

Albert's head after he was found during his second escape exploit, rather battered and with his cap badge missing.

were very few and far between, and for reasons quite obvious would-be escapers able to speak German were afforded priority. After some debate by the Escape Committee it was decided in the end that the initial attempt using Albert was to be made by Lt. William 'Blondie' Mewes, R.N.V.R. The German-speaking Bill Mewes, a strong and determined character who as a boy seaman had traversed Cape Horn under sail, was ready and eager to go, so no more time was wasted.

The following Thursday, bath day, was a tense time for one and all. Came the call to Showers Parade, Albert's separate parts were bundled up into towels before the Room formed up outside in the usual columns of three. As always they were counted twice before being marched up the road for their weekly session in the bath-house. Bathing was a communal affair in which the kriegies luxuriated, jostling good-humouredly amidst the clouds of steam for prime position under the shower-heads. The omnipresent guards took little notice of these cavortings, so the scenario was very near perfect. Under cover of the boisterous horseplay Lt. 'Blondie' Mewes climbed a low wall built inside the bath-house and concealed himself in the small lavatory it hid. His bundles of food and clothing were passed over to him, and then began a nerve-wracking wait for darkness, when the coast might hopefully be clear for him to set out on his long trek to freedom.

Everything depended, however, on his room-mates being able to assemble Albert as they hustled about getting dressed, and afterwards use him to fool the guards. It was an exercise in co-operation and cover-up, to say nothing of *legerdemain,* with every practised member of the team skilfully playing his part. Albert was successfully put together, (his head could be fitted in a very few seconds) and supported on the arms of Worsley and Staines, he 'got fell in' outside. It can hardly be difficult to imagine the tension as the guard began his count, but none of it was permitted to show. The usual banter went on, with the kriegies cracking jokes and lighting cigarettes. But the first count went perfectly, and the number having been found to be correct, the order was given to move off. The column was halted inside the camp gates, and another head-count was made by a German officer moving slowly along the ranks. The deception worked yet again, and when the bath party was finally dismissed Albert was hustled into the hut for swift dismantling and concealment. The Room was jubilant, but the jubilation was tempered by anxiety over the fortunes of Bill Mewes, crouched in the smelly little W.C. waiting for darkness to fall, under constant threat of discovery.

It was a threat which, fortunately, did not materialise, and in fact 'Blondie' Mewes got away. But Albert's work was far from over. The prisoners were mustered outside and counted no fewer than three times a day, and it had been determined that Mewes should be afforded a minimum of four days grace in which to get well clear of the camp before his absence became known. So, Albert was assembled to take his place in the ranks and was 'counted' — in broad daylight — more than a dozen times before, on the fifth day, he was finally dismantled and hidden away *pro tem.*

That this most skilfull and brilliant deception ended disastrously had nothing to do with the part played by Albert. Worsley's pencil-drawn identity card 'photograph' with its 'official' German Eagle and swastika overstamp never failed to pass scrutiny, nor did the travel permit and other of his papers executed by the forgery team. Indeed, Bill Mewes reached the Baltic port of Lubeck and had managed to get into the docks before the guards at Marlag 'O' were allowed to discover that one of their charges was missing. Having wormed his way into the dockyard, Mewes sneaked aboard a Swedish cargo vessel and placed himself at the mercy of the captain. Vastly to his dismay, his plea for sanctuary was flatly refused and it must, after all he had thus far achieved, have come as a crushing blow to be so close to freedom, and yet so far. But Mewes was an extraordinary man, set firm in the mould of Bruce's spider. He slipped aboard another Swedish ship, and once again asked its skipper to take him back to neutral home port. A second flat refusal left him in desperate straits. His escape kit was exhausted and now, with no food and no money, he was virtually trapped in the docks and was soon picked up by the ever-vigilant Gestapo and sent back to Marlag 'O' after having been absent for almost a month. In the interim, he was subjected to intensive interrogation as to the means by which he escaped, but he never revealed the secret of Albert, and Albert remained secure.

In hindsight, the conduct of these Swedish captains seems odd to say the least. At a time when many of their countrymen worked unceasingly to help and comfort prisoners-of-war, these two actively contrived to exacerbate the plight of one such unfortunate. They were asked to run no risk, merely to extend a helping hand.

Following Bill Mewes' return to the camp, Albert was secreted away to remain in hiding during a cooling-off period. The totally-inexplicable escape had thrown the Germans into a panic. Vigilance was greatly increased by a drafting-in of more guards and more dogs and more rigorous *appels,* or counts. Inevitably, however, the passage of time brought an easing of the Germans' rage and frustration, and it was suggested then that Albert be resurrected for use in a second escape. He had, after all, performed superbly and it certainly wasn't his fault that Bill Mewes had been betrayed at Lubeck, so why not bring him back into play?

The proposal was put to Worsley by the inmates of another room, who asked if they might borrow Albert. Their request was agreed by the Escape Committee, and there followed a period of intensive training. Albert was taken out of dry dock, dusted and freshened up, and put to a series of tests and trials. When his second team handlers and minders had proved themselves proficient in the job, the Escape Committee convened again and issued a go-ahead.

As we have seen, each Room was semi-autonomous within the larger context of its hut, which in turn was semi-autonomous within a cohesive whole which embraced the entire camp and all of its inmates. So, having agreed to lend Albert and to train the leasors in his use, Worsley and his Room mates could only stand by as onlookers to the drama which ensued.

As before, Albert was operated by a team of eight or nine. When the relevant shower party was mustered, the man who had taken Worsley's place was carrying Albert's head bundled up in a bath-towel. Another was wearing the reinforced greatcoat, and two others each carried a leg. The original team, including Bill Mewes, lounged around outside, 'casual' observers of the well-rehearsed performance. Everything went well. Albert was smuggled into the bath house, the bathers had their showers, and the escaper got himself into the lavatory. Albert was smoothly put together, and took his place in the ranks outside, and passed the first count with flying colours.

Then, just as Albert's operators were congratulating themselves and the party was about to march off, one of the guards felt an urgent call of nature. He shouted for a temporary halt, and hurried towards the lavatory. The kriegies watched with sinking hearts, waiting for the yell of alarm which must sound when the guard opened the lavatory door. The escaper was swiftly dragged out, dressed in the clothes of a Polish workman. The guards rushed around like ants, in a scene like that of a comic opera. They counted, and counted once more. One prisoner too few was not impossible, but one too many — *Mein Gott!* It was beyond all credibility! They counted yet again — always including Albert — and, defeated, finally resolved to march the whole contingent back into the camp and so place the onus of resolving the mystery on their commanding officer.

Once the party was secured inside, and the German commandant had taken over, he ordered his officers to check every man *individually*. They were separated from the ranks three by three, and submitted to a thorough search. This took place in the German compound, watched from behind the high wire by a sickened Worsley and the rest of the prisoners. It was an extraordinary spectacle. In the melee of hustle and confusion, Albert's handlers performed a minor miracle of deception and sleight-of-hand. They managed completely to dismantle Albert and disperse his various parts among kriegies towards the rear of the column. But although they could assimilate his greatcoat and cap and his bath-towels stuffing, they could not hide his head, and when it finally reached the end of the column Worsley's perfect masterpiece was dropped ignominiously into the dust and back-heeled away to the rear so that no one man was left in possession.

Impossible, of course, for the Germans not to spot it. The head was pounced upon, and so the elements of the plot were exposed.

German reaction to the revelation was both triumphant and derisory. The camp commandant mustered the inmates, and delivered an admonitary address in which he poured scorn on their efforts. Such childish capers, he said, were stupid and totally ineffective, doomed before they even began. He went on to warn the captives that any further attempt at escape would doubtless end in a similar fiasco. The bellows of laughter prompted by this statement rose to a mighty roar when his anger prompted him to express himself idiomatically.

'You Britisch offitsers,' he yelled, 'you think that we Schermans know f*** nottings, but we Schermans know f*** *all!*'

The thunderous roars of hilarity which greeted this unfortunate *gaffe* put the joke more firmly upon the commandant because of course he was unaware that Albert had already worked spectacularly well in the matter of Bill Mewes' escape, and that had it not been for the malign coincidence of one guard's pressing need to defecate, he must surely have worked again. John Worsley puts it into a nutshell: 'Albert's downfall was due to German bowels, and not to German brains.'

The original physical essence of Albert — that is to say, his head — was appropriated by the Germans and never seen again. Later, Worsley made a replica, but lacking that vital necessity to get every tiny detail absolutely and perfect correct, one wonders if any substitute could ever be quite the same.

# CHAPTER 9
# MILAG NORD

The weeks and months which followed Albert's denouement passed uneventfully. 1944 was drawing to a close. Life in the camp went on, but with energies now concentrated on fitness and survival, rather than escape. The prisoners knew from grapevine intelligence that it was a matter of not much time before the Allies triumphed over Germany, and came to set them free. So life assumed a kind of normality. Educational classes went on, with Worsley teaching drawing and painting, and rather than waste effort on digging tunnels, the kriegies just settled down to wait. It was a period of relative inactivity before the final release, and their future now virtually secured, the prisoners' became increasingly reflective. So far as Worsley was concerned, he nurtured a regret which still exists: because of a strong wartime antipathy to all things German, he never took advantage of a perfect opportunity to learn the language. He realises now that had he attended the classes, he could have become quite proficient in the tongue.

In the meantime, Christmas approached, with its festive demand of traditional celebration. This time, there were no bottles of schnapps to be bartered for and buried and lost in iron-frozen ground, but the inmates of Marlag 'O' still yearned for a Christmas roast even *sans* the cheering cup with which to toast the food. Each separate Room within the huts competed to excel, and the competition assumed esoteric proportions. In the last few days of the run-up to Christmas, the inmates of Worsley's Room received a visit from one of their neighbours. This officer of His Majesty's Royal Navy was offering a considerable barter price in exchange for one big fat cat, or alternatively, two medium-size cats. Those feral felines which sneaked into the camp were never kept as pets, because food with which to feed any animal was needed by the human kind, and cats were regarded as pretty fair game. At a distance in time of almost half a century, Worsley recalls nothing of this deal except that it actually was proposed, and whether or not an adjacent Room enjoyed a Christmas dinner of roast tabby remains a matter for speculation. The writer would wager that they *did*. In today's Britain there are fortunately very few of us

MILAGE NORD.
'Horse racing' in one of the huts. The horses moved along by throwing dice.

left who have ever experienced actual deprivation, the constant daily problem of never having quite enough to eat; of never enjoying the ease and comfort which only a full belly can bring.

For the captives of Marlag 'O', Christmas '44 came and went, and its aftermath brought a dramatic increase in the size and frequency of Allied air raids. Huge numbers of Flying Fortresses filled the skies overhead in follow-my-leader tight formation. British Lancasters adopted much looser patterns, like gigantic gaggles of geese. German opposition was crumbling, and the kriegies saw far fewer 'planes shot down. Nearby Bremen, and Hamburg — fifty miles away — were being quite literally razed to the ground. There was hardly ever a day when the rumbling drone of heavy bombers did not fill the air, and now there were attacks by fighter aircraft. American Mustangs and British Mosquitoes roared over the camp in low-level swoops, intent on straffing anything that moved along the surrounding roads.

One of these fighters, a British Mosquito, did the prisoners a very bad turn. After 'buzzing' the camp at rooftop height, all the time waggling his wings to cheer and encourage the inmates, the pilot banked away and disappeared from sight behind a stand of pines. Almost immediately, there was a harsh staccato rattling of machine-gun fire, and the kriegies raised a cheer. Had they been able to see what was happening, there would have been agonised groans of dismay. The camp's supply of bread was delivered weekly in a horse-drawn cart, and it was this which the pilot had blown to pieces. Marlag 'O' had no bread for a week.

It was about this time that Worsley decided that his on-the-spot sketches of life in captivity were not going to be complete without some depiction of Milag Nord. But, though less than one mile away, the camp for Merchant Navy prisoners was just as unreachable as if it had been a thousand. The only traffic between the two camps was when one of the Marlag's men fell in need of expert surgical attention. Common ailments and illnesses were either treated by the inmates themselves, or by a German army doctor. After racking his brains for a solution to his problem, the artist hit upon a plan. The symptoms of, say, appendicitis would be difficult to fake convincingly, and even if he succeeded in doing so the necessity would remain for the operation *to be seen to be done*. No, an abdominal job was not on — not least, of course, because Worsley wished to be up and about during the period of his convalescence, not lying flat on his back.

The bright idea which finally came to him involved his committing himself to an operation which, though not dangerous, would be painful in the extreme. He decided to sacrifice that small portion of anatomy traditionally excised from all male infants of the Jewish persuasion, and

MUSICAL NEGRO SAILOR IN HOSPITAL.

Negro seaman P.O.W. Milag Nord. April 44

the decision having been made he began to complain of trouble with that appendage. As before with Albert, R.N., the Machievellian plan worked, and Worsley was taken under escort for attention at Milag Nord in the capable hands of its resident surgeon.

Major R. Harvey of the Royal Army Medical Corps 26th General Hospital, was one of the War's unsung heroes. He was captured whilst on active service in Greece, having deliberately chosen to stay in order to care for the severely wounded overtaken by a German advance. How he came to wind up in Milag Nord is something we now do not know, but his presence there is recorded for posterity by Worsley's portrait of him, executed *in situ* and now the property of the British Imperial War Museum.

Having suffered the unnecessary operation, and his ultimate goal achieved, Worsley employed the time so afforded to wander around Milag Nord and record his impressions with pencil and paper. He was fascinated by what he saw, a fascination reflected in the many sketches he made, some of which appear in these pages. Milag Nord was a polyglot community of something like ten thousand souls. Masters and crews, and even passengers, of every merchant ship ever sunk by Germany throughout the course of the war, as many nationalities of creed and colour as ever sailed under one flag. The prison camp of Milag Nord was absolutely unique. It was a microcosm of human society encircled by barbed wire, and inhabited by people of diverse cultures. In practice, it was a miniature world set down near a village somewhere in Germany.

Its effect on Worsley was utterly to astonish. Accustomed as he was to the well-defined parameters of Royal Navy discipline, the observance of certain taboos and inviolable Rules of Honourable Behaviour, the scene in Milag Nord resembled a Tower of Babel, but the way in which it was all made to work was spectacularly ingenious. Milag Nord had its own monetary system, paper money printed by the Germans as a sort of anodyne, known and accepted as laager marks. These were freely exchanged in return for goods, or services.

The various national and ethnical factions incarcerated in Milag Nord tended to specialise in certain areas of 'business'. In the very broad term, each ethnic group ran its own operation and collected its laager marks and exchanged them for those services which they needed but did not provide, and in spite of anomalies, the system ran smoothly. There were huts in which to get a haircut and a shoe-shine, and huts which were sort-of pubs, and a hut which housed a (male) brothel. There was a considerable range of shops. There was a hut which housed a race-track several metres long, all of it carefully man-made, where the progress of plywood horses was determined by throws of dice, and this was but one of several 'casinos'. Wherever there are people who wish to gamble, and no matter what form the stakes, there will always be those who remain much wiser and are prepared to cater for them. Modern psychology might define the gambling which went on at Milag Nord as a seeking after mental relief, a substitute for actual physical escape, and any such diagnosis might well have been accurate.

So far as is known, there was never any attempt to escape from captivity at Milag Nord, although the prospect of doing so was very much less daunting than it was at the camp down the road. The Germans had not troubled to surround the place with a very deep water-filled ditch, although the wire was quite formidable. Faced with the problem of

GAMBLING 'TABLES'.
One of the many gambling 'tables' (the roulette wheel made from a bicycle wheel) where 'Lager marks' change hands and where seamen of all nationalities congregated in the afternoons.

getting out, the inmates of Marlag 'O' would have seen Milag Nord as a 'piece of cake'. There was a simple reason for this. The merchant seamen had no *need* to break out. They were taken out every day to work as labourers on surrounding farms, and it was this restricted freedom which made life in Milag Nord so very different from that in Marlag 'O'. Regular contact with the civilian population provided ample opportunity for barter on a massive scale and also, of course, for widespread pilfering. The merchant seamen traded their Red Cross goodies for fresh vegetables and chickens and ducks and for the various 'raw materials' with which to make artefacts which were traded in turn for more desirables. Milag Nord was less of a prison camp than a complex industrial machine based entirely on private enterprise, and managed by entrepreneurs. This must have given rise to internecine disputes, but in the interests of a larger peace, the guards would doubtless have turned a blind eye.

ASIAN SAILORS.
Some of the Asian sailors kept rabbits; note the design of the hutch.

Worsley was impressed by his sample of slice of life in Milag Nord, but on the whole, he found it offensive. It was inevitable in any such rat-race that the weakest must go to the wall, and he much preferred the spirit of fellowship which prevailed in Marlag 'O', with its pooling of all food from Red Cross parcels scrupulously supervised by a duly-appointed Catering Officer. The experience reinforced a conviction that free-wheeling anarchy was an inferior substitute for the order incumbent in good Naval discipline. Nevertheless, his painful sacrifice had not been made in vain. He recorded a vivid pictorial chronicle which stands forever unique

# CHAPTER 10
# THE MARCH TO LUBECK

The New Year of 1945 occasioned a celebration much more significant than the usual traditional event. Victory for the Allied armies had become a certainty, with the Axis forces in disarray. Clandestine radio sets built by prisoners all over Germany daily brought fresh news of massive advances on every front; of the Russians from the east, and of British and American from most other points. Excitement was intense, and not confined to the captives. In a desperate last-ditch stand, their captors planned to move them north to be held as hostages in the forthcoming peace negotiations. It was a scheme with small hope of success, but the Germans had their backs to the wall and the commandant of Marlag 'O' ordered his charges to make themselves ready to evacuate the camp, and prepare for a march to Lubeck.

The order prompted feverish activity among the prisoners. In the absence of any kind of transport, decisions had to be made. What to pack, and carry on their backs, and what to leave behind? Lubeck lay eighty miles to the north, rather more than an easy stroll quite apart from restrictions and harassment sure to be encountered along the way. Also, there would be no cosy overnight halts with field-kitchens all set up and shelter with blankets and such provided. They would need to carry everything necessary in order just to survive. Some officers elected to opt out of the march, and began a hurried digging of caverns underneath the huts with the intention of hiding themselves until they were liberated. The majority, which included Worsley, adopted a philosophical stance. Secure in the knowledge that their trials were almost over, they prepared to say goodbye to the cage which had been their home for so long.

Each man was posed with a personal dilemma as to which of his few but precious possessions took precedence over the rest. Worsley's greatest regret was that he had to abandon the ceiling-board portrait of Captain

*Captain Micklethwaite's portrait was brought home by the Army when Marlag 'O' was over-run, and later returned to him at his home in Surrey. It hangs now in the farm of his son, Mr Richard Micklethwaite, near Chepstow in Gwent.

Micklethwaite. It was left *in situ,* looking down on the Room.* However, and fortunately for us, he stuffed three canisters made from empty KLIM milk tins with his paintings of the V.C.s, and his numerous Marlag 'O' sketches. He carried the canisters, in addition to his gear, over eighty long weary miles and got them, eventually, back home to England.

The trek from Westertimke to Lubeck, which took the better part of two weeks, resembled a training exercise designed to toughen up young troops. Worsley and three others from his Room managed to spend one fairly comfortable night when they commandeered a small pig-sty, though they shared it with the biggest fattest pig that either of them had ever seen. Their sleep was punctuated by loud snorts and grunting, but at least they were warm and dry. The nights spent shivering in fields and ditches curled up against the cold and the rain were otherwise relatively peaceful, but each and every dawn brought new fear of harassment by their own compatriots. Marauding ground-attack aircraft of the Allies dominated the skies, and some of the pilots seemed over-enthusiastic. They shot up everything in sight, and the long straggling columns from Marlags 'O' and 'M' must have looked like fair game. At a speed of several hundred miles an hour they obviously could not see the home-made White Ensign which the prisoners had draped over the one little horse-drawn cart, and could not recognise the khaki battledress uniforms.

If one particular pilot did spot the signs, he spotted them much too late. Worsley regards himself as having been lucky that he and the rest of his Room habitually marched near the head of the column. It was thanks to this forward position that they escaped death or injury when the marchers were attacked one morning by a solitary low-flying Hawker Typhoon. As both kriegies and guards dived for cover, those near the head of the column escaped the hail of machine-gun bullets by leaping into a roadside ditch, but those towards the rear became aware of the danger those vital few seconds too late, and some fell dead or wounded. Tragically, among the six Britishers killed outright was an elderly R.N. captain, veteran of two World Wars. Captured very early in the war, the old man had spent five long years as a prisoner and had been looking forward with joy to imminent reunion with his wife and family.

The tragedy came close to being repeated not long afterwards, when the marchers were bedded down in the shelter of a pine wood. Allied night-fighters ranged overhead, but the forest afforded effective cover. Effective cover, that is, until 'some anonymous simpleton was careless enough to show a light. The light was seen, and swooped upon, and suddenly the surrounding branches were spattered and furiously ripped by a barrage of gun and cannon fire. Miraculously, and fortunately, the only casualties on this occasion were suffered by the trees.

To those taking part, the march seemed endless. During pauses for rest along the way they bartered with the local civilians for ancient handcarts or wheelbarrows, and especially rickety old prams. Anything on wheels which could be pushed, or pulled, and used to lighten the loads otherwise back-packed or carried in bags. A section of this bizarre procession is accurately depicted in Worsley's *The March To Lubeck,* painted later from his sketches and now in the Imperial War Museum.

One reason why the eighty-mile trek took so long is that the prisoners themselves were determined to move as slowly as possible, in the hope of being overtaken by the van of an Allied thrust. Uncertain as to what awaited them at Lubeck, they were hoping for liberation before they reached that place. To this end, they were deliberately obstructive, disrupting their daily progress by any means they could. The guards might have used harsher measures to hurry their charges along, but with the smell of defeat in their nostrils, they probably feared the consequences. They had no knowledge, as yet, of the penalty soon to be paid by that one of their number responsible for the murder at Marlag 'O', but all must have known what early retribution to expect should the prisoners be subjected to maltreatment. The writing was on the wall.

When in spite of all their delaying tactics the kriegies did finally reach Lubeck they were herded, together with Polish and other foreign prisoners, into a large military barracks alongside an autobahn. Although the war was in its final stages, literally the last few days, pressure from the Allies continued unremittingly. But the Germans fought to the end, and the barracks often reverberated to the thunder of anti-aircraft guns from two batteries situated in fields adjacent to the perimeter wire. In the middle of one fine morning during these last few days, the prisoners lined the barracks fence to witness what for them was the very last fighting of World War Two.

When a flight of RAF fighter-bombers suddenly appeared in the sky, the gun crews rushed to action stations and put up a barrage of fire. This time, however, the RAF was not just passing. They commenced a dive to attack, and the ack-ack batteries were utterly destroyed. Resounding cheers from the front-line spectators were taken up by the ranks behind and echoed throughout the barracks.

Those cheers were to herald The End. Still standing at the wire only twenty minutes later, and looking down the autobahn, Worsley experienced an unforgettable sight. Over a distant rise, there gradually materialised the shape of a tank. First, a man standing up in the cockpit with field-glasses held to his eyes, Then, the gun, and the turret, and the tracks. This first leviathan was followed by another, and another, until the whole autobahn was filled with tanks and transport vehicles. The 11th Armoured Division had arrived. The head of this huge snake of arms and armour veered into an enormous field and began to circle like a Wild West wagon train, curling up on itself 'just like a dog settling down in a basket'. (These last are John Worsley's words.) A young German soldier who was watching with Worsley carefully laid down his gun, and put up his hands in surrender. His comrades quickly followed suit and then, for the kriegies, the war was over.

# CHAPTER 11
# JOHN WORSLEY'S PEACE

The first days of freedom, with the roles of guards and prisoners having been reversed, were celebrated at Lubeck in some style. Worsley commandeered a small bus, and drove parties of ex-kriegies on sightseeing tours of the old town. This revelling in their new-found liberty went on for four hectic days before the merrymakers were finally mustered, and ferried to the nearby airfield at Blankensee ready to be flown home to England. While they were waiting there, German aircraft of the Luftwaffe were flying in to land and surrender and one of these, a Messerschmitt 109, provided the onlookers with an unusual spectacle. When the fighter had taxied to a halt and the pilot climbed out, he was followed by a second officer and then, astonishingly, a third. How all three managed to pack themselves into a single-seater remains a mystery.

But the repatriates themselves were scarcely less crowded on their flights back home. They were flown in Lancaster bombers, 25 passengers to each 'plane, rather like sardines in a tin, taking turns to crawl over each other for a view from either cockpit or bomb-aimer's position. Worsley was lucky. His turn to catch a glimpse of what lay beneath came just as the Lancaster flew low over the English coastline. It had started gently to rain, and that first sight of the fresh green fields of England was, he admits, an experience charged rather high with emotion.

The fleet of Lancasters taking part in the airlift landed at an RAF station somewhere in the Midlands, and if the homecomers expected a heroes' welcome, they were swiftly disenchanted. They were immediately pounced upon by a battery of very formidable ladies in nurses' uniforms each armed with a can of anti-nit powder. Almost smothered with the stuff, and only after a thorough de-lousing, were they allocated to huts. Not unnaturally, that first evening 'at Home' was spent in a local pub, and Worsley recalls his feelings as he took his first long pull at a foaming pint: he had never ever imagined, he says, that beer could taste so good.

Over the next few days, the ex-prisoners of Marlag 'O' were gradually despatched each to his own divisional port, or depot. Worsley returned to Portsmouth, where he was kitted out with new R.N. battledress, identity papers and travel warrant, and given two weeks leave which he spent with his father in London. Most of the ex-prisoners were demobilised soon after this terminal leave, but Worsley's services were somewhat special, and his time in uniform was to be extended by a further six months. He was given no further 'rough duty' — he was allowed to live ashore in a small studio flat in London, in Baron's Court — but he remained under Naval discipline. He still had work to do. His job was to paint the portraits of certain Very Important Persons, last but not least of whom was General (later Field Marshal) Montgomery of Alamein. These 'official' portraits are listed in chronological order.

Rear Admiral Sir Cloudesley Robinson K.C.B., D.S.O, painted in a room at the Admiralty. Major General Hamilton Wilkie Simpson C.B., D.S.O., Royal Marines, painted at the R.M. barracks in Chatham. Admiral Sir John Cunningham K.C.B., M.V.O., C-in-C Mediterranean, painted in Naples at the 'Villa Emma', a house which once belonged to Lady Hamilton and the one in which she used to entertain Nelson. Admiral Sir Max Kennedy Horton G.C.B., D.S.O., prominent submariner 1914–1918 and C-in-C Western Approaches 1939– 1945, painted in a room at the Admiralty. Eng. Rear Admiral Sidney Oswell Frew C.B., one of the very few senior officers to have been promoted from the lower deck, painted at Chatham dockyard.

One other painted by Worsley during this period, although not 'official', is interesting because of the character it portrays. Brigadier Peter Young, D.S.O., M.C., Commanding Officer No. 3 Commando, was a very large and extremely tough person.

The final portrait painted by Worsley whilst he was still an officer of the Royal Navy was that of General Montgomery. He was given short notice of the commission, and when one morning a large black flag-flying Rolls-Royce swept into the narrow road behind Baron's Court railway station and stopped at the door of his little flat he was caught, as they say, on the hop. He hastily bundled his traps together, easel and paints and canvas and brushes, and only when he was seated in majesty behind the driver did he realise with dismay that he had forgotten to pocket his wallet, with all of his papers, money, etc. Fortunately, the oversight presented no problem. He was smoothly conveyed to London airport, driven straight up to Monty's private 'plane, and whisked to the general's HQ in Germany.

It is now widely recognised and accepted that in addition to his having been a great wartime leader, Field Marshal the Viscount Montgomery K.G., G.C.B., K.C.B., C.B., D.S.O., was a strange and complex man. Having spent a comfortable night in one of Schloss Ostenwalde's beautiful rooms, Worsley met the great man in his study the following morning. It was a meeting tinged with awe. The highest-ranking soldier in the British Army made it instantly clear to the humble R.N. lieutenant that he was a very busy man, and issued his orders in brief clipped phrases.

'Right. I can sit for you on Monday, and Tuesday. On Wednesday, one of my aides will substitute for me, wearing my uniform. I will sit for you again on Thursday.'

End of (one-sided) conversation. As the portrait developed, however, so did Worsley's confidence, and he began to ask himself *why* he should feel overawed by the Field Marshal's imperious manner. So prompted by his resentment, he presumed to venture a question:

'Sir, have you yourself ever done any painting?'

Monty's reply, typically abrupt, encouraged no further discourse. *'No. Never had the time.'* Strongly suggesting that if he *had* had the time, Worsley's present efforts — along with those of any other artist — would be entirely superfluous.

Worsley's encounter with Monty afforded him an insight into yet another facet of the soldier's intriguing character. In Monty's study were six birdcages, each containing a chirruping canary. At one of the sittings, one of the cages had been left open, permitting its occupant to flutter around the room. Seeing it as a rather nice touch, the artist painted a canary into the portrait, a little yellow bird sitting on top of its cage. This small but noticeable feature might well cause future generations viewing Worsley's painting to be seriously misled, as indeed was the artist himself. When he was flown back to England, again in Monty's private 'plane, he was accompanied by one of his A.D.C.s. In conversation during the flight, Worsley mentioned the birds and expressed an opinion that anyone who cared for such tiny creatures must have *some* quality of human kindness, after all. The A.D.C. laughed.

'What? Don't you believe it! He only keeps them to test for gas!'

The trip home from Germany offered another surprise when the pilot made a detour and flew down low over Marlag 'O', in order to give Worsley an aerial view of the camp which had been his home. The ex-inmate thought he was taking one last look, but an imminent event proved him wrong.

Shortly before he was finally demobilised, Worsley was employed by Ealing Studios in an advisory capacity on the making of a film entitled *The Captive Heart*. The main scenes were set in a prison camp, and the genuine location chosen for the filming was none other than Marlag 'O'.

It was a weird situation made even more bizarre by the fact that even as the film was being made in Marlag 'O', in the central compound previously occupied by the German Admin. block, that part of the camp which comprised Marlag 'M' was being practically employed as a prison for German S.S. officers.

Once filming was well under way, this strange anomaly assumed even greater proportions. As with all film locations, the daily scene at Marlag 'O' appeared to be chaotic. The endless activities involved a veritable host of production people, technicians, actors and extras, and obviously, some of these last were dressed in authentic German uniforms. Almost inevitably, one of the German S.S. prisoners grasped the opportunity to engineer an escape. He somehow inveigled himself through the wire which separated the camps, mingled with the spurious S.S. officers taking part in the film, and calmly walked off the set. He succeeded in making his escape, and was never seen or heard of again. So it was that the Marlag saga ended in irony.

It was the end, too, of Worsley's days in the Royal Navy. He was demobilised at Portsmouth with an outfit of civilian clothes and a travel warrant for the journey back to Civvy Street. As he stepped through the gates of the depot he was waylaid by those ubiquitous touts who habitually pestered ex-servicemen to sell their smart new gear.

Once a sailor, always a sailor. He responded in Naval terms.

# INDEX